The MESSIANIC PSALMS

T. Ernest Wilson

Books by T. Ernest Wilson

Angola Beloved
The Farewell Ministry of Christ
God's Call to Special Service
God's Sacred Secrets: *Mystery Doctrines of the New Testament*
Men of the Mountains and Valleys
1 Thessalonians (*What the Bible Teaches* Series)

The MESSIANIC PSALMS

T. Ernest Wilson

GOSPEL FOLIO PRESS
P. O. Box 2041, Grand Rapids MI 49501-2041
JOHN RITCHIE LTD., Kilmarnock, Scotland
40 Beansburn, Kilmarnock, Scotland KA3 1RH

Cover design by J. B. Nicholson, Jr.

Originally published in 1978 by Loizeaux Brothers, Inc.

Co-published by Gospel Folio Press
P. O. Box 2041, Grand Rapids MI 49501-2041
and John Ritchie Ltd.
40 Beansburn, Kilmarnock, Scotland KA3 1RH

Gospel Folio Press ISBN 1-882701-28-3
John Ritchie Ltd. ISBN 0-946351-70-8

Printed in the United States of America

To the memory of
the intrepid pioneer evangelists and Bible teachers
of the last generation, who left home, comfort, and safety
to bear the Light to dark places of the world
for love of Christ,
this volume
is respectfully dedicated.

Contents

Introduction

On the resurrection day, the risen Christ met two disciples on the way to Emmaus, and from Moses and all the prophets He expounded to them the things concerning Himself. As a result, their whole outlook was changed. Later they declared: "Did not our heart burn within us, while He talked with us by the way, and while He opened to us the scriptures?"

At eventide, in the Upper Room, He appeared to the gathered disciples and said: "These are the words which I spoke unto you, while I was yet with you, that all things must be fulfilled, which were written in the law of Moses, and in the prophets, and in the psalms, concerning Me." He then opened their minds to understand the Scriptures.

There are a number of psalms which speak of the Person and work of the Lord Jesus Christ. They are called Messianic psalms obviously because they speak of the Messiah. The question may be asked: "How can we recognize a Messianic psalm?" The answer would be: where there is a reference to the Messiah in a psalm, and it is applied to Christ and expounded in the New Testament. Sometimes a whole psalm applies to Christ, e.g., Psalm 22. Sometimes a paragraph, e.g., Psalm 40: 6-10. Sometimes several verses, e.g., Psalm 69:4, 9,

21. Sometimes a single verse, e.g., Psalm 41:9.

It is obvious that some of the psalms are occupied entirely with the Person and the thoughts and feelings of our Lord, while others clearly refer to the experience of the psalmist, and then there is included an isolated reference to the Messiah. Psalm 69 is an example. When David exclaims: "O God, Thou knowest my foolishness, and my sins are not hid from Thee," he obviously is referring to himself (v. 5). But when he says: "They gave me...gall for my meat; and in my thirst they gave me vinegar to drink" (v. 21), and these words are applied to Christ in Matthew 27:34, 48, they are clearly Messianic. So we must be careful to distinguish between the spiritual experience of the writer of the psalm and the prophetic reference to Christ Himself.

We need to pay careful attention to the exhortation of Paul to Timothy: "Study to show thyself approved unto God, a workman that needeth not to be ashamed, rightly dividing the word of truth."

While keeping in mind this rule, that a quotation in the New Testament from a psalm, which applies it to the Lord Jesus, confirms it as Messianic, there are three psalms which are exceptions. They are obviously Messianic but are not quoted in the New Testament:

Psalm 24 speaks of the King of Glory.

Psalm 72 outlines the millennial reign of Christ.

Psalm 89 expounds the Davidic covenant fulfilled by David's greater Son, the Messiah. We therefore include them in the list of Messianic psalms.

It is to be noticed that the references to the Messiah in the psalms do not follow in sequence or in chronological order. Psalm 2 is an introduction to the whole collection, giving a prophetic outline of the official glories of the Messiah. Psalm 40 refers to His incarnation; Psalm 22 to His crucifixion; Psalm 16 to His resurrection. In our exposition we shall follow the chronological order in the life of our Lord. There are sixteen Messianic psalms and we shall consider them in the following sequence: (1) Psalm 2: The Official Glory of the Eternal Son; (2) Psalm 40: The Incarnation; (3) Psalm 91: The Temptation; (4) Psalm 41: The Betrayal; (5) Psalm 22: The Crucifixion; (6) Psalm 69: The Trespass Offering; (7) Psalm 16: The Resurrection; (8) Psalm 68: The Ascension; (9) Psalm 45: The King-Bridegroom; (10) Psalm 24: The King of Glory; (11) Psalm 110: The Priest-King-Judge; (12) Psalm 8: The Last Adam; (13) Psalm 72: The Millennial Reign; (14) Psalm 89: The Davidic Covenant; (15) Psalm 102: The Unchangeable One; and (16) Psalm 118: The Headstone of the Corner.

It is our earnest prayer that our understandings may be opened to see the things concerning Him in these precious psalms, and that the Holy Spirit who inspired them will help us to interpret them, and apply them with power to our hearts.

1
Psalm 2
Official Glories of the Eternal Son

PSALM 2

1 Why do the heathen rage, and the people imagine a vain thing?
2 The kings of the earth set themselves, and the rulers take counsel together, against the LORD, and against His anointed, saying,
3 Let us break their bands asunder, and cast away their cords from us.
4 He that sitteth in the heavens shall laugh: the Lord shall have them in derision.
5 Then shall He speak unto them in His wrath, and vex them in His sore displeasure.
6 Yet have I set My king upon My holy hill of Zion.
7 I will declare the decree: the LORD hath said unto Me, Thou art My Son; this day have I begotten Thee.
8 Ask of Me, and I shall give Thee the heathen for Thine inheritance, and the uttermost parts of the earth for Thy possession.
9 Thou shalt break them with a rod of iron; Thou shalt dash them in pieces like a potter's vessel.
10 Be wise now therefore, O ye kings: be instructed, ye judges of the earth.

11 Serve the LORD with fear, and rejoice with trembling.
12 Kiss the Son, lest He be angry, and ye perish from the way, when His wrath is kindled but a little. Blessed are all they that put their trust in Him.

OFFICIAL GLORIES OF THE ETERNAL SON

Psalms 1 and 2 are linked together in the Hebrew Bible. They are an introduction and a preface to the Psalms as a whole. Attention has been drawn to the fact that the first psalm begins with a beatitude, and the second ends with a beatitude. Together they form an admirable introduction to the Messianic psalms. In the first we see Christ's moral glory; in the second, His official glory. In the first, He is the happy Man, occupied with a book, a tree, and a river; in the second, He is God's King, destined to rule the nations with a rod of iron. In the first, we have His humanity; in the second, His deity. The common theme of both is the glory of God's beloved Son, the Messiah, who, in spite of all the anarchy and wickedness in the world, will one day occupy the throne of world dominion.

Psalm 2 is quoted seven times in the New Testament: Acts 4:24-28; 13:33; Hebrews 1:5; 5:5; and Revelation 2:27, 12:5; 19:15. All of these references are applied to the Messiah, our Lord Jesus Christ, giving us our authority for calling it a Messianic psalm. There are four official Messianic titles in the psalm, one in each section: The Anointed (v. 2); My King (v. 6); My Son (v. 7); the Lord (v. 11).

AN OUTLINE OF PSALM 2

Psalm 2 has 12 verses, divided into four sections of three verses each. There are four speakers, one in each section:

1. The voice of rebellion—man in revolt (vv. 1-3).

2. The reply of Jehovah—God in His wrath (vv. 4-6).

3. The revelation of the Son (vv. 7-9).

4. The Spirit's call to reconciliation (vv. 10-12), the answer of the Holy Trinity to the anarchy of man.

1. THE VOICE OF REBELLION—MAN IN REVOLT (PS. 2:1-3)

"Why do the heathen rage, and the people imagine a vain thing? The kings of the earth set themselves, and the rulers take counsel together, against the Lord, and against His anointed, saying: Let us break their bands asunder, and cast away their cords from us."

The Apostle Peter applies these words to the crucifixion in Acts 4:27-28, "For of a truth against Thy holy child Jesus, whom Thou hast anointed, both Herod, and Pontius Pilate, with the Gentiles, and the people of Israel, were gathered together, for to do whatsoever Thy hand and Thy counsel determined before to be done." This is the primary application of the passage, but it has a prophetic application as well.

Here we have a fourfold coalition of power united against Almighty God and His Christ. First, the united nations; secondly, "the people," the nation of Israel; thirdly, organized government represented by Herod; and finally, judicial power represented by Pontius Pilate. The confederacy at the cross foreshadows another at the end. They imagine a vain thing—that they can overthrow God! The words "take counsel" and "set themselves" indicate the deliberate adoption of a policy, the passing of a resolution. It is the overthrow of law and order, the underwriting of the slogan, "God is dead."

The law of God in the Bible and all rules concerning morals and marriage are to be rejected. Man is the maker of his own destiny and "situation ethics" is to be the rule of life. All bands and cords are to be thrown away and modern man is to be liberated from all restraint. Even today there are straws in the wind which indicate what will happen at the end when all the bars are down. It starts in the home where the child instead of the parent rules. It continues in the school, where it is illegal to discipline with the rod, and where evolution and Hegelian philosophy is taught by infidel teachers and professors. It increases in the social sphere, where the gay generation openly claims license for unnatural sin, abortion has been legalized, and unisex breaks down the distinction between man and woman. Then it reaches into the sphere of government: sex scandals, graft, and corruption, from the policeman on the street to the judge on the bench, penetrating into the highest echelons of government.

If these things take place while the Holy Spirit and the Church are here as restrainers (2 Thess. 2:7), what will it be when they are removed? Today the mystery of iniquity is already working, but it will be revealed in all its lurid wickedness when the avalanche breaks forth.

The French Revolution of 1798 was a little foretaste of it, when a harlot was enthroned in Notre Dame, and again in 1917 after the Bolshevik Revolution, when millions were liquidated and godless atheism took over. It was repeated in Red China when Mao and communism swept the country, and kangaroo courts accounted for the lives of untold millions of victims.

The second Psalm points forward to that day when a satanic trinity, the two wild beasts of Revelation 13, backed by the devil himself, will proclaim a decree prohibiting the worship of God and His Christ, our Lord Jesus Christ (2 Thess. 2:3-4; Rev. 13:4-8; 12:17). Those that refuse to obey, to carry his mark, and to worship the image of the man of sin will be executed. This will be the climax of the work of the united nations of the earth and the final fulfillment of the first section of this psalm.

2. THE REPLY OF ALMIGHTY GOD (PS. 2:4-6)

"He that sitteth in the heavens shall laugh: the Lord [Adonai]

shall have them in derision." It is a terrible portent when God laughs. The very idea that puny man can defy the One who has the universe in the palm of His hand, is supremely ridiculous. Ballistic missiles and laser beams are as children's toys to Him. He knows their secrets and more.

"Then shall He speak unto them in His wrath, and vex them in His sore displeasure." "The wrath" in the book of Revelation is a technical term, indicating the final series of judgments in the Great Tribulation. The seal judgments are those that men bring on themselves by their own folly, such as the building up of nuclear arms, which one day will be unleashed, with a large portion of the world's population wiped out and material resources destroyed. The trumpet judgments are mainly satanic, when men will reap the wages of sin. They are similar to the plagues of Egypt described in Exodus 7-12. But the bowls or vial judgments are the wrath of God, the concentrated anger of the Almighty poured out on the seat of the beasts and their followers.

The climax of all this is: *"Yet have I set My king upon My holy hill of Zion."* This is God's unalterable purpose, and nothing on earth or in hell can thwart it. In the first section of the psalm, He is the Anointed, but here He is King. This points forward to that day foretold by the prophets, when, after dealing with the enemies of God at Armageddon, He will enter the city at the head of His victorious army and occupy the hill and the house. He will be the King-Priest on the throne of His father David (Ps. 24 and 110; Zech. 6:13). God regards this in His purpose as already accomplished.

3. THE REVELATION OF THE SON (PS. 2:7-9)

"I will declare the decree: the Lord hath said unto Me, Thou art My Son; this day have I begotten Thee." This is one of the decrees of the Godhead in eternity past, here revealed for the first time by the Son. It is one of the greatest Messianic pas-

sages in Holy Scripture. The eternal Sonship of Christ is one of the most vital, basic doctrines of the Word of God. It is denied by many heretical cults, but should be held and valued by all those who know and love our Lord Jesus Christ. This is the great passage on which the doctrine is based. Another term, used only by the Apostle John, is "the Only Begotten Son," *the monogenes.* John uses the term five times.

Some theologians teach that the word "begotten" must not be understood as referring to any act in time but to what they term an "eternal generation." The word "day" is explained as "eternity." Taken in this way, the eternal Sonship of Christ is safely guarded. But others maintain that the three places in the New Testament where the words are quoted give the explanation. In view of the definiteness of the term "this day," it would seem difficult to define it as synonymous with eternity. It must refer to some special act in what we know as "time." Here we must be on our guard against those who say that He only became the Son of God at His incarnation and who deny His eternal Sonship.

The statement in verse 7 is in two parts: *"Thou art My Son,"* the decree in eternity past. That is an eternal relationship. *"This day have I begotten Thee,"* is Messianic, quoted in three contexts in the New Testament. Notice them carefully.

Acts 13:32-34 states, *"And we declare unto you glad tidings, how that the promise which was made unto the fathers, God hath fulfilled the same unto us their children, in that He hath raised up Jesus again; as it is also written in the second psalm, Thou art My Son, this day have I begotten Thee. And as concerning that He raised Him up from the dead, now no more to return to corruption, He said on this wise, I will give you the sure mercies of David."*

Verse 33 clearly refers to His raising up to Israel, His incarnation, and verse 34 to His resurrection. Between the two statements, we have the quotation from Psalm 2:7: *"Thou art My Son; this day have I begotten Thee."* Thus it is linked with His incarnation and His resurrection.

In Hebrews 5:5, it is quoted in connection with His exaltation as our High Priest. *"So also Christ glorified not Himself to be made an high priest; but He that said unto Him, Thou art My Son, to day have I begotten Thee."*

In Hebrews 1:5-6, the quotation is linked with His second advent. No angel receives worship, but when He brings again the First-Begotten into the world, He says: *"Let all the angels of God worship Him."* So it was that at His birth He was saluted as Son by the angels (Lk. 1:35), by His Father at His baptism (Lk. 3:22), and at His transfiguration (Lk. 9:35).

To summarize: the two statements of Psalm 2:7 indicate "Thou art My Son," a unique eternal relationship; and "This day have I begotten Thee," an official salutation, a term linked with His incarnation, baptism, transfiguration, resurrection, priesthood, and Second Advent. Kenneth Wuest, who does not believe that it refers to His incarnation, but to His resurrection, comments, "The reference is not to entrance into life, but to entrance to an office."

After Sonship comes Heirship: *"Ask of Me, and I will give Thee the nations for Thine inheritance, and the uttermost parts of the earth for Thy possession. Thou shalt break them with a rod of iron; Thou shalt dash them in pieces like a potter's vessel."* This points forward to the day when He shall return to reign. The shepherd's rod, symbolizing authority and rule, to His people will be a golden scepter, but to the rebel nations at Armageddon will be a rod of iron (Rev. 2:27; 12:5; 19:15; Ps. 110:2).

4. The Spirit's Call to Reconciliation (Ps. 2:10-12)

The admonition of the Spirit is to the kings and judges of earth, the executive and judicial branches of government. True wisdom is in reconciliation while there is time and before the judgment of God falls on the unrepentant.

"Kiss the Son" (v. 12). The kiss in Scripture is a symbol of various attitudes. In Luke 7:38, it is a sign of repentance. The

poor woman who came into the house of Simon and stood behind Jesus, did five things: she wept, she washed His feet with her tears, she wiped them with the hairs of her head, she kissed His feet, and she anointed them with the ointment. The tears and the kiss were an evidence of true repentance. Our Lord said, "Her sins, which are many, are forgiven; for she loved much."

The kiss is also a token of forgiveness. In Luke 15:11-24, the prodigal came back home to his father, and after his confession, received the kiss of forgiveness, a ring, a robe, shoes on his feet, and a welcome-home banquet.

But here it is an expression of homage and loyalty (Gen. 41:42; 1 Sam. 10:1). The ARV renders the expression, "with trembling, kiss His feet."

It is interesting to notice that two words for "son" are used in the psalm. In verse 7 it is *ben,* but in verse 12 it is *bar.* The first is the Jewish word, cf., Benjamin; the second is the Gentile word, cf., Bar-abbas. Why the difference? The first is His relation to God as the Son of His right hand; the second His relation to the Gentile powers referred to in the psalm. At the crucifixion they cried, away with Him, give us Bar-abbas. The use of the word here would be a stab at their conscience. Judas gave Him the kiss of hypocrisy and treachery, but here the admonition is to kiss the Son in true contrition and repentance. If the psalm was written at the time of the Absalom rebellion, what a tragic local reference it has!

The psalm ends with the beatitude: "Blessed are all they that take refuge in Him!" Indeed, there is no other sure refuge when Heaven comes to settle Earth's accounts.

2
Psalm 40
The Psalm of the Incarnation

PSALM 40

To the chief Musician, A Psalm of David.

1 I waited patiently for the Lord; and He inclined unto me, and
heard my cry.
2 He brought me up also out of an horrible pit, out of the miry clay,
and set my feet upon a rock, and established my goings.
3 And He hath put a new song in my mouth, even praise unto our
God: many shall see it, and fear, and shall trust in the Lord.
4 Blessed is that man that maketh the Lord his trust, and respecteth
not the proud, nor such as turn aside to lies.
5 Many, O Lord my God, are Thy wonderful works which Thou hast
done, and Thy thoughts which are to us-ward: they cannot be reck-
oned up in order unto Thee: if I would declare and speak of them,
they are more than can be numbered.
6 Sacrifice and offering Thou didst not desire; mine ears hast Thou
opened: burnt-offering and sin-offering hast Thou not required.
7 Then said I, Lo, I come: in the volume of the book it is written of
me,

8 I delight to do Thy will, O my God: yea, Thy law is within my heart.
9 I have preached righteousness in the great congregation: lo, I have not refrained my lips, O Lord, Thou knowest.
10 I have not hid Thy righteousness within my heart; I have declared Thy faithfulness and Thy salvation: I have not concealed Thy lovingkindness and Thy truth from the great congregation.
11 Withhold not Thou Thy tender mercies from me, O Lord: let Thy lovingkindness and Thy truth continually preserve me.
12 For innumerable evils have compassed me about: mine iniquities have taken hold upon me, so that I am not able to look up; they are more than the hairs of mine head: therefore my heart faileth me.
13 Be pleased, O Lord, to deliver me: O Lord, make haste to help me.
14 Let them be ashamed and confounded together that seek after my soul to destroy it; let them be driven backward and put to shame that wish me evil.
15 Let them be desolate for a reward of their shame that say unto me, Aha, aha.
16 Let all those that seek Thee rejoice and be glad in Thee: let such as love Thy salvation say continually, The LORD be magnified.
17 But I am poor and needy; yet the Lord thinketh upon me: Thou art my help and my deliverer; make no tarrying, O my God.

THE PSALM OF THE INCARNATION

In the study of the Messianic psalms, we are repeatedly confronted with the difficult problem of determining that which refers to the author and that which refers to Christ. Very often the psalmist, under the Spirit's power and inspiration, is lifted beyond the limits of his own personality, to present the Person of the Messiah. The difficulty is greatly increased when only a part of the psalm is quoted in the New Testament with reference to our Lord, and the remainder of the psalm would seem to refer to the psalmist himself. This is especially so in Psalm 40.

In this psalm there are three verses which are quoted in Hebrews 10:5-7 as having been addressed to the Father by our Lord on His coming into the world, the quotation being taken from the Septuagint version. There is no doubt that these words of the psalmist found their complete fulfillment in our Lord.

But in the latter part of the psalm, there are two statements which make it difficult to see a personal utterance of the Messiah. They could be true of David but not of Christ. First, the personal confession of iniquities in verse 12; and secondly, the imprecations of verses 14-15. Some would meet this difficulty by saying that the spotless Victim was so taken hold of by our sins that He confesses them as His own. There is no question that, in voluntary, vicarious atonement, our Lord bore our sins in His own body on the tree, but we never find Him confessing personal sin as David did when he said: *"Mine iniquities have taken hold upon me, so that I am not able to look up; they are more than the hairs of mine head."*

Then again, the imprecatory exclamations seem to be the very antithesis of our Lord's cry on the cross: "Father, forgive them; for they know not what they do." But we can make no mistake in applying the central portion of the psalm, verses 6 to 10, quoted in Hebrews 10 and applied to our Lord, and the rest of the psalm to David's personal experience.

AN OUTLINE OF PSALM 40

1. David's desolating experience and deliverance (vv. 1-5).
2. The Incarnation of the Messiah (vv. 6-10).
3. David's prayer for help and comfort (vv. 11-17).

1. DAVID'S DESOLATING EXPERIENCE & DELIVERANCE (PS. 40:1-5)

Historically, the first part of the psalm could be applied to

David's experience during the Absalom rebellion or to the dark episode in his life when he sinned against God in the matter of Bathsheba, and his cry of repentance described so vividly in Psalms 51 and 32. As Jeremiah literally sunk in the deep mire of the pit in which King Zedekiah had allowed him to be cast by the princes, so David had a similar spiritual experience. This seems to have occurred often in his life: when he was hunted by Saul, when he fled to Gath, when he was rejected and living in the cave of Adullam, and when his sons rebelled against him. Then he was not able to look up (v. 12); his cry of distress went up (v. 1); he was brought up and cleaned up (v. 2); he was set up and his feet placed upon the rock (v. 2). Then he was tuned up, with a new song placed in his mouth, even praise unto God. As he contemplated all of God's wonderful works and thoughts towards him, he tells us that they could not be reckoned up. These elevating experiences, which David had, are true of every redeemed soul today. We, too, can add, that one day soon we are going to be caught up! What a joy it is for the saint to have the solid rock of ages for his feet, the new song of redemption in his mouth, and the law of God in his heart!

2. THE INCARNATION OF THE MESSIAH (PS. 40:6-10)

This great central section is in four parts, with the incarnation clause in the center: "Lo, I come" (v. 7). Note:

a) The inadequacy of the Levitical sacrifices (v. 6).
b) The opened, digged ear of the Servant (v. 6).
c) The predictions of the sacred Scriptures (v. 7).
d) The law hidden in the inner shrine of His heart (v. 8).

The Inadequacy of the Levitical Sacrifices (v. 6). "Sacrifice *[zebach]* and offering *[minchah]* Thou didst not desire; mine ears hast Thou opened: burnt offering *[olah]* and sin-offering *[chataah]* hast Thou not required." The four Hebrew words used cover the principal offerings of the Levitical code. *Zebach is* a general term for all the eucharistic sacrifices, the peace, votive, and thank offerings. *Minchah is* the meal offering with which is connected the drink offering. *Olah is* the burnt offering. *Chataah* refers to the expiatory sacrifices, the sin and trespass offerings. All pointed to the death of Christ on the cross.

As we study the ancient sacrifices described in Leviticus 1-7, we find that they are divided into two groups. The first are "sweet savor" offerings, consisting of the burnt, meal, and peace offerings. The second are sin and trespass offerings. The sin offering had reference to sin against God, violating His holy character, and called for judgment. The trespass offering added to this the injury done to man, for which reparation had to be made.

The offerings were different, but all set forth various aspects of the Person and work of Christ. The burnt offering was the highest and most important. In all the other sweet savor offerings, parts were offered on the altar and went up to God; but the other parts were divided among the people and the priests, and became the food of the people of God. But the whole burnt offering was completely consumed on the altar. There was something in the sacrifice of our Lord Jesus Christ which only God Himself could understand and appreciate in all its fullness.

The meal offering presents His moral glory and sinless humanity linked with His deity. The peace offering speaks of that One who made peace by the blood of His cross. The sin offering portrays the sinless One who was made sin for us, and the trespass offering tells of the Sufferer who was wounded for our transgressions, and who in love restored that which He took not away.

It is a mistaken view that the sacrificial system of Israel was merely ritual. The sacrifices were God's kindergarten to the nation, pointing forward to a coming Messiah who was to suffer and die for the sins of the nation, indeed, for the whole world. The offerings were profoundly educational and spiritual. But alas, they degenerated from this ideal into mere external performances. Then God expressed His repudiation of them. (See 1 Sam. 2:12-17; 15:22; Isa. 11-12; Amos 5:21-24; Prov. 15:8; Mal. 1:7-8.)

In the Mosaic sacrificial system, millions of animals were sacrificed and rivers of blood flowed. The ox, goat, sheep, lamb, and turtle dove were sacrificed upon the altar. All had meaning, and all pointed to the cross. This was the picture-book stage of Israel's history. But Psalm 40 renders a twofold verdict: "Sacrifice and offering Thou didst not desire...Burnt offering and sin offering hast Thou not required." The Epistle to the Hebrews gives us the reasons.

The Opened, Digged Ear of the Servant (v. 6). "Mine ears hast Thou opened." The Hebrew word for "opened" is *karah.* It is translated eleven times "digged," once "opened," and once "pierced." In this passage it would seem to have the latter meaning, and refers to the Hebrew servant of Exodus 21:1-6 and Deuteronomy 15:12-18. In Exodus 20, we have the Law and the altar, and this is followed in chapter 21 with the law of the Hebrew bond servant. This is the order and teaching of Psalm 40:6-10. Our Lord voluntarily took the bondsman's form (Phil. 2:7). The reason for the Hebrew slave's bondage was either debt or bankruptcy. To liquidate this, he could sell himself and his service for six years or until the year of jubilee. All this is a picture of man's ruin by sin and of a groaning creation.

Note two distinct periods of service in the story. The first six years were compulsory; then there was a crisis and a decision. Brought to the judge, a public legal transaction takes place. "And if the servant shall plainly say, I love my master, my wife, and my children; I will not go out free: then his master shall bring him unto the judges; he shall also bring him to the door, or unto the doorpost; and his master shall bore his ear through with an awl; and he shall serve him for ever."

In the first part of his service, his motive was love to his master; in the second, there is an additional love, that to his acquired wife and children. The first part of his service was compulsory, but the second was voluntary, motivated by love. Verse 3 says: "if he came in by himself" (literally, with his body) "he will go out with his body." The doorpost was where the blood was sprinkled at the passover in Egypt, and where the written Law was placed when they reached the land of Canaan (Deut. 6:9; 11:20). The veil that covers the typical teaching here is very transparent and radiant.

It is a wonderful picture of the incarnation and of those permanent wounds, the tokens of His love to His Church, which were made upon Him at Calvary. In a coming day, the brand of the Beast will be on the forehead or hand of his dupes. Here, however, it is on the ear, the place where the Master's voice is heard. In Hebrews 10, the ear is changed to "a body hast Thou prepared Me." Why is this? When the ear of the servant is pierced as a token of love, God gets the whole body.

"Then said I, Lo, I come"—The Incarnation. Here we have a conversation between the Father and the Son. That blessed One, who was ever in the bosom of the Father, declares His coming into the world of time and space. It was a voluntary, self-conscious act. Of no other could this be said. Yet note how the Trinity is included in this act:

a) It was His own act of compassion (Jn. 8:42, 44; 6:38; 16:28; Heb. 2:14-16).
b) It was the Father's act of love (Jn. 8:42; Gal. 4:4; 1 Jn. 4:9).
c) It was the Spirit's work of power (Mt. 1:18-20; Lk. 1:35).

The incarnation is a profound mystery (Mt. 11:27; 1 Tim. 3:16). By that act, Jesus became God manifest in flesh. The Apostle John uses just four words to describe the incarnation: "The Word became flesh." Luke, on the other hand, goes into detail, using 2,500 words. While assuming sinless humanity,

Jesus never for a moment ceased to be God. There can be no gap or hiatus in deity. Instead of subtraction, there was addition. To complete, essential Deity, with all its attributes, was added a holy, perfect, human body. "Veiled in flesh the Godhead see."

Some have said that He didn't understand His identity or His mission until His baptism in Jordan, when the Spirit descended and abode upon Him. Others have speculated that He only learned who He was by the study of the Old Testament Scriptures. But He certainly knew His identity and mission at twelve years of age, when He said to Mary and Joseph, who were seeking Him in the Temple: "Wist ye not that I must be about My Father's business?" While it transcends our poor finite comprehension, we prefer to agree with the sentiment of the poet:

No less majestic at His birth, as on the throne supreme;
His hands upheld the rolling spheres while Mary held up Him.

In Him we see Omnipotence wrapped in swaddling bands, Omniscience though a little babe, Omnipresence dwelling in the City of David.

The Predictions of the Sacred Scriptures (vv. 7-8). "In the volume of the book it is written of Me, I delight to do Thy will, O My God." This can be nothing else but Messianic prophecy in the Old Testament Scriptures. From the *proto-evangelium* in the Garden of Eden, the promise of the Seed of the woman (Gen. 3:15) till the promised advent of the Messenger of the Covenant in Malachi 3:1, there is a long series of predictions of the coming of the Messiah. To cite just a few:

The Promise: The Seed of the woman (Gen. 3:15).
The Place: Bethlehem, not Nazareth (Micah 5:2).
The Person: The Child virgin born, the Son given (Isa. 7-9).
The Program: Outline of His public ministry (Isa. 61:1).
The Passion: (Ps. 22; Isa. 53).

The Period: At end of 69 weeks Messiah cut off (Dan. 9:26).
The Priesthood: After the order of Melchizedek (Ps. 110).

Over all these Old Testament references could be written: "I delight to do Thy will, O My God" (Ps. 40:8). When He was tired and hungry and thirsty at Sychar's well, He could say to the disciples, "My meat is to do the will of Him that sent Me, and to finish His work" (Jn. 4:34). In His great high-priestly prayer in John 17 He prayed: "Father, I will that they also, whom Thou hast given Me, be with Me where I am; that they may behold My glory." This is deity speaking to deity. But in His agony in dark Gethsemane, He cried, "Father, if Thou be willing, remove this cup from Me: nevertheless not My will, but Thine, be done" (Lk. 22:42). His whole life was a carrying out of His Father's will and in this was His delight.

The Law Hidden in the Inner Shrine of His Heart (v. 8). The first clause of the new covenant is: "I will put My laws into their hearts, and in their minds will I write them" (Heb. 10:16). This was true, first of all, of our Lord. Just as the tables of the Law were hidden in the Ark of the Covenant, so the ancient Scriptures were hidden in His heart.

It is interesting to notice the use He made of Holy Scripture in His public ministry. He set the stamp of His authority on the writings of Moses (Mt. 5:18), of Daniel (Mt. 24:15), of David (Mt. 22:43), and of Isaiah (Lk. 4:17). At His temptation by Satan in the wilderness, He quoted three times from the book of Deuteronomy. On the cross He used the words of Psalm 22 amid the darkness, "My God, My God, why hast Thou forsaken Me?" And just before He released His spirit, He cried, "It is finished," a quotation from the last verse of the same psalm. Truly the Word of God dwelt in Him richly. He is the blessed Man of Psalm 1. "His delight is in the law of the Lord; and in His law doth He meditate day and night."

Fivefold Preaching to the Great Congregation (vv. 9-10). As a result of the work of Christ in His incarnation and His sacrificial death on the cross, a fivefold message goes out to the great congregation, in fact, to all mankind:

Righteousness: This is the subject of the Epistle to the Romans—the righteousness of God—how God can be both just and the justifier of the ungodly.

Faithfulness: He is the God who is "utterly dependable" (Heb. 11:11, *Phillips*), and the Lord declared that steadfastness, even if it meant death on a cross.

Salvation: Salvation in its three tenses of deliverance from the penalty, power, and presence of sin, expounded in Ephesians 2.

Lovingkindness: The length and breadth and depth and height of God's love, opened up for us in the Upper Room ministry of Christ in John 13-17.

Truth. Love is always balanced by truth, as John teaches us in his three Epistles.

3. DAVID'S PRAYER FOR HELP AND COMFORT (VV. 11-17)

The third section of the psalm goes back to David's personal experience. It consists of a prayer. First, conviction and confession: "Innumerable evils have compassed me about: mine iniquities have taken hold upon me, so that I am not able to look up; they are more than the hairs of mine head: therefore my heart faileth me" (v. 12). Then his cry for help (v. 13). Finally, salvation and deliverance come. "Let all those that seek Thee, rejoice and be glad in Thee; let such as love Thy salvation say continually, the Lord be magnified!"(v. 16).

Psalm 40 in Hebrews 10:5-7

The writer of Hebrews quotes the Septuagint version of the psalm. This is the Greek version of the Old Testament translated in Alexandria in the third century BC. The Holy Spirit sanctions the translation.

There is no discrepancy. It is simply an evidence of inspiration. The change of, "Mine ears hast Thou opened," to "A body hast Thou prepared Me," is apparently an allusion to the Hebrew servant of Exodus 21. The pierced ear is an evidence that the whole body is dedicated.

The Hebrews passage emphasizes:

a) The will of God (v. 7).
b) The work of Christ (v. 12).
c) The witness of the Holy Ghost (v. 15).
d) All is sealed by the new covenant (vv. 16-17).

The old system is set aside by the offering of the body of Jesus Christ once for all (v. 10). Then twice we have the final word, "forever." "After He had offered one sacrifice for sins forever, sat down on the right hand of God" (v. 12). "For by one offering He hath perfected forever them that are sanctified" (v. 14).

This is the fulfillment of the great Messianic prophecy of Psalm 40, and the climax of teaching concerning the incarnation and vicarious atoning sacrifice of the Saviour on Calvary's cross as recorded in the Epistle to the Hebrews.

3
Psalm 91
The Psalm of the Temptation

PSALM 91

1 He that dwelleth in the secret place of the most High shall abide
under the shadow of the Almighty.
2 I will say of the LORD, He is my refuge and my fortress: my God;
in Him will I trust.
3 Surely He shall deliver thee from the snare of the fowler, and from
the noisome pestilence.
4 He shall cover thee with His feathers, and under His wings shalt
thou trust: His truth shall be thy shield and buckler.
5 Thou shalt not be afraid for the terror by night; nor for the arrow
that flieth by day;
6 Nor for the pestilence that walketh in darkness; nor for the de-
struction that wasteth at noonday.
7 A thousand shall fall at thy side, and ten thousand at thy right
hand; but it shall not come nigh thee.
8 Only with thine eyes shalt thou behold and see the reward of the
wicked.
9 Because thou hast made the LORD, which is my refuge, even the

most High, thy habitation;
10 There shall no evil befall thee, neither shall any plague come nigh thy dwelling.
11 For He shall give His angels charge over thee, to keep thee in all thy ways.
12 They shall bear thee up in their hands, lest thou dash thy foot against a stone.
13 Thou shalt tread upon the lion and adder: the young lion and the dragon shalt thou trample under feet.
14 Because he hath set his love upon Me, therefore will I deliver him: I will set him on high, because he hath known My name.
15 He shall call upon Me, and I will answer him: I will be with him in trouble; I will deliver him, and honor him.
16 With long life will I satisfy him, and show him My salvation.

THE PSALM OF THE TEMPTATION

Psalms 90 and 91 are the introduction to the fourth Book of Psalms. This Book, or subdivision, consists of seventeen psalms, from Psalm 90 to Psalm 106. It corresponds to the book of Numbers and is a commentary on the experience of the children of Israel in the wilderness. Moses is the author of Psalm 90 and probably of Psalm 91 as well. There are many expressions in both psalms similar to or identical with those used by Moses in his farewell address to Israel in Deuteronomy 32 & 33. Moses' name occurs seven times in this section of the Psalms.

There is a vivid contrast between Psalms 90 and 91:

Psalm 90	*Psalm 91*
600,000 overthrown	Two survivors—Caleb and Joshua
Judicial punishment	Divine preservation
Funeral dirge	Doxology of victory
Tragedy and gloom	Triumph and victory
"Dead March" in *Saul*	Hallelujah chorus in *Messiah*

Both begin with a divine dwelling place. Psalm 90 ends with a sevenfold prayer. Psalm 91 ends with a sevenfold promise. It may be noted that the seven promises are the answers to the seven prayers.

AN OUTLINE OF PSALM 91

1. Divine protection (vv. 1-4). It is fourfold, as seen below.
2. Satanic perils (vv. 5-13). There are ten dangers.
3. Divine promises (vv. 14-16). There are seven.

In this psalm, sinful man is permitted to hear the sweet converse between the three Persons of the ineffable Trinity: the Spirit (v. l); the Son (v. 2); the Spirit (vv. 3-13); the Father (vv. 14-16).

The psalm can be applied in a threefold way: a) Messianic (vv. 9-13) where the temptation is prefigured (Mt. 4:6; Lk. 4:10-11); b) a portrait of Joshua and Caleb, survivors of the wilderness tragedy; and c) as the believer today.

1. DIVINE PROTECTION (VV. 1-4)

If we find our refuge in the Secret Place, who will be our companion? The Spirit mentions four names of God, a galaxy of titles, each with a specific precious meaning. *The Most High—El Elyon,* was used by Melchizedek (Gen. 14:19), and by Daniel (4:24). It is used mostly in relation to Gentiles (Deut. 32:8). Shaddai—Almighty, was used by Jacob and Job. Some say it is derived from *shad,* the breast. It speaks of God as the Provider, the All-Sufficient One. *Jehovah*—the covenant-making and covenant-keeping God, is also included in the introduction to this psalm, as is *Elohim*—the Creator (as in Gen. 1:1).

Thus these verses could be read thus: He that dwells

(makes his home) in the secret place of *El Elyon,* shall abide (lodge) under the shadow of *Shaddai.* I will say of *Jehovah,* He is my refuge and my fortress, my *Elohim:* in Him will I trust.

These four magnificent titles of God, describing His majesty, glory, power, compassion, and tenderness, are the resource and hiding place for every timid and tried child of God. There are four descriptions of this hiding place for the saint: a) a secret place, known only to God and His children; b) a mighty fortress, impregnable to the enemy; c) A soldier's equipment—a shield and buckler (perhaps a coat of mail, Eph. 6:11-18); and d) a bird's nest, where we are covered by the wings of the mother bird. This is a beautiful simile used of creation, the Passover, the Tabernacle, Ruth, by David in the Psalms, and by our Lord in Matthew 23:37. Moses would see the eagle in the desert of Sinai, with its mighty wings and claws and beak protect its young in the nest.

I recall hearing an African say, "The mother hen has four calls: for food, when in danger, for warmth, and to call her chicks to be with her." So the Lord would call out to us.

We have the same idea of shelter in the wings of the cherubim over the mercy seat in the holiest in the Tabernacle, and in the Shekinah cloud of glory covering the Tabernacle.

Theodore Beza, the reformer and Bible translator, when dying, went back to the three personal pronouns of Psalm 91:2: my refuge, my fortress, my God, in Him will I trust. Moses, Elijah, David, Paul, and John were well acquainted with this secret place. It is available for us, too.

In the days of the persecution of the Covenanters in Scotland, a group of humble saints were having a secret meeting on the moors. A scout suddenly reported, "The soldiers are coming!" The venerable Alexander Peden, the preacher for the "hill folk," dropped on his knees and cried: "O Lord, cover old Sandy and his flock with the shadow of Thy wing." Then a thick mist came down and blanketed them from view, and the soldiers passed on, unable to find God's people.

2. SATANIC PERILS (VV. 5-13)—THE WILDERNESS EXPERIENCE

Ten enemies are mentioned in three categories:

Weapons of the enemy. The arrow by day and the terror by night come suddenly upon us. The snare and the booby trap are like the attacks of Amalek and Moab. Later, the maledictions of Balak and Balaam also sought to ambush God's own.

Bodily sickness. The noisome pestilence that walks in darkness, and the destruction that wastes at noonday portray the calamities that overcome us. The book of Numbers describes the various plagues that overtook the people in the wilderness, all of them brought on by their own folly and sin. In the rebellion of Korah, 14,700 died (Num. 16:49). In the plague that followed their sin with the women of Moab, 24,000 died (Num. 25:9). At the end of forty years, out of the 600,000 men that left Egypt, only two survived—Joshua and Caleb.

Wild beasts. The lion, the adder, and the dragon are mentioned. All three are used as figures of Satan in the Scriptures. The lion devours (1 Pet. 5:8); the serpent or adder is the most subtle (Gen. 3:1); the dragon is the persecutor (Rev. 12:13).

In this section of the psalm is the passage used by Satan at the temptation of our Lord in the wilderness. Satan used the same tactics as he did to Eve in the garden of Eden. He misquoted the Word of God, and then he added to it.

The Temptation of Christ (Mt. 4:1-11; Lk. 4:1-13): The first act of our Lord after His baptism in Jordan, at the beginning of His public ministry, was to go into the wilderness to be tempted by the devil. Mark says: "He was driven by the Spirit into the wilderness" (Mk. 1:12). This does not mean that there was compulsion against His will. As the last Adam, He was to be tested where the first Adam had failed. But the conditions are in startling contrast.

The first temptation had to do with *appetite;* Christ was desperately hungry. "If Thou be the Son of God, make these stones bread" (Mt. 4:3), but He answered, "Man shall not live by bread alone, but by every word that proceedeth out of the mouth of God"(v. 4). The temptation of Eve was in a garden of delight, a perfect environment, but our Lord was tested in a desert after He had fasted for forty days. The temptation in Eden was addressed to the body, soul, and spirit; likewise our Lord's.

The second temptation was addressed to *ambition.* "The devil taketh Him up into the holy city, and setteth Him on a pinnacle of the temple, and saith unto Him: If Thou be the Son of God, cast Thyself down" (v. 6). Then comes the misquotation from Psalm 91:11-12, "For it is written, He shall give His angels charge concerning Thee: and in their hands they shall bear Thee up, lest at any time Thou dash Thy foot against a stone." Here are Satan's tactics with the Word of God. He left out the words, "to keep Thee in all Thy ways," and he added the words, "at any time." The devil is never more dangerous than when he quotes or misquotes the Word of God!

Our Lord's answer: "It is written...thou shalt not tempt the Lord thy God" (v. 7). To throw Himself down from a pinnacle of the Temple, to impress the multitude always looking for a thrill, was not one of the ways directed by His Father.

The third temptation concerned *adoration.* "The devil taketh Him up into an exceeding high mountain, and showed Him all the kingdoms of the world, and the glory of them; and said unto Him, All these things will I give Thee, if Thou wilt fall down and worship me. Then said Jesus unto him, Get thee hence Satan; for it is written, thou shalt worship the Lord thy God, and Him only shalt thou serve" (Mt. 4:8-10).

There are some important considerations concerning the temptation of our Lord which it is vital to understand clearly.

There is an important difference between Adam and the Lord Jesus Christ. Adam was created, and prior to his sin was innocent. Our Lord was the uncreated eternal Son of God and was holy, not merely innocent. We must always bear in mind that He was God incarnate. We must not separate His two distinct natures—His essential deity and His perfect sinless manhood. Scripture tells us that He was sinless: John says: "In Him is no sin" (1 Jn. 3:5). Peter says: "Who did no sin" (1 Pet. 2:22). Paul says: "Who knew no sin" (2 Cor. 5:21). He was the Lamb without blemish (1 Pet. 1:19).

He was in all points tempted like as we are, yet sin apart (Heb. 4:15). In Him there was no enemy to open the door, no evil fallen nature on which the enemy could work.

In spite of these plain statements of Scripture, some would say that while He did not sin, yet He could have sinned, else it was not a real temptation. This is very dangerous ground and raises some serious questions as to the Person of Christ. Some would cut the Gordian knot by saying that He was tempted in the realm of His humanity and therefore could have failed. But this again is dividing the two natures. To say that the GodMan could have sinned or could have fallen is blasphemous!

At the same time, He suffered being tempted. The temptations were real. His holy, sensitive nature revolted at the suggestions which were made to Him. There are two kinds of temptation. James speaks of one: "Every man is tempted, when he is drawn away of his own lust, and enticed" (Jas. 1:14). This is true of men, but not of our Lord.

Another meaning is testing. Abraham was tested when God asked him to offer his son as a burnt offering. Every girder in a bridge is tested, not hoping it will break, but to prove that it can stand the strain. Pure gold can be tested by fire. The fire does not make it gold, but demonstrates that it is gold. Every gold coin can be tested by ringing on a metal disc and by weighing. Is it a sham test of those that have no alloy? It is possible for a city to be besieged although impregnable. Is it a sham siege? A sinless personality would be able to feel the force of temptation even more than we do. It was not a sham fight between His holy nature and Satan. Therefore we hold to an impeccable Christ.

The method He used in overcoming Satan is available to us all: "It is written…it is written…it is written." The sword of the Spirit, the Word of God with its two edges, is like Goliath's sword. David said: "There is none like that; give me it" (1 Sam. 21:9). If our Lord could drive back the enemy with just one book of the Bible, surely we may do it with sixty-six!

Psalm 91:13 can therefore confidently declare: "Thou shalt tread upon the lion and adder; the young lion and the dragon shalt thou trample under feet." These words seem to have a direct reference to Genesis 3:15. The seed of the woman shall bruise the serpent's head. Satan was soundly defeated at the temptation in the wilderness, but it was at the cross that his head was crushed and his power over death annulled (Heb. 2:14). Paul could comfort the saints at Rome with the words, "The God of peace shall bruise Satan under *your* feet shortly" (Rom. 16:20). Praise God! We are included in the victory!

3. Divine Promises (vv. 14-16)

Here we have the voice of God the Father. Seven times we have the words, "I will." These are things He did for His beloved Son, but also what He will do for His people. They are not spoken to the trusting soul, but of him to others by the Father. This makes the utterances very impressive. Notice that the seven promises are the answers to the seven prayers of Psalm 90:14-17.

His love. All is traced back to God's love and our response to it. This was true, first of all of Christ and His love to His

Father, mentioned many times in John 13-17. We love Him because He first loved us. The New Testament speaks of six people whom Jesus loved. He loved Martha, her sister, and Lazarus; the rich young ruler; the Apostle John—the disciple whom Jesus loved; Paul could say: "He loved me and gave Himself for me" (Gal. 2:20). As the seventh, we can put in our individual names and say: "He loved me, blessed be His name."

His Name. "I will set him on high, because he hath known My name" (v. 14). This could be applied to the Lord Jesus in His resurrection and exaltation to God's right hand. But we, too, when we know and enjoy the meaning of the names at the beginning of this psalm, can be lifted out of this dreary world and enter into the peace and rest of the secret place of the Most High.

Prayer. "He shall call upon Me and I will answer him." This was true of the secret prayer life of our Lord when He was here below, so beautifully outlined in Luke's Gospel. We can also gladly testify to answered prayer. Again and again the Lord has heard our cry and answered in the nick of time.

Trouble. "I will be with him in trouble." Job said: "Man ...born of a woman is of few days, and full of trouble" (Job 14:1). But in contrast, the Saviour said: "Let not your heart be troubled: ye believe in God, believe also in Me" (Jn. 14:1). What a comfort it is to have the presence of the Lord with us in our trouble.

Honor and deliverance. "I will deliver him, and honor him." The Word declares: "Them that honor Me I will honor, and they that despise Me shall be lightly esteemed" (1 Sam. 2:30). This is illustrated in the lives of Moses, Joseph, and Daniel, and in the experience of many others since.

Long life. "With long life will I satisfy him." In spite of the seventy to eighty years predicted as frail man's life span in Psalm 90:10, Moses lived 120 years, and at the end, his eye was not dim nor his natural force abated. Joshua lived 110 years. Caleb at 85 asked for a tough task; he took on the three sons of Anak and captured Hebron, the royal city (Josh. 14; Eph. 6:2-3). We might ask, If long life is promised to obedient children, why do some submissive children die at a young age. The answer in part may be found on the tomb of a young believer in the Catacombs: "He lived long enough." Rebels never live long enough to fulfill the purpose for which they were made. Only the obedient child lives "long enough."

And show him My salvation. Salvation has three tenses: past, present, and future. There is deliverance from the penalty, power, and presence of sin.

A venerable Scottish brother preached a sermon with three heads:

a) l John 1:7—"The blood of Jesus Christ cleanseth us from all sin." He exclaimed: "There's my sins awa'."

b) Psalm 55:22—"Cast thy burden upon the Lord, and He shall sustain thee." He cried: "There's my burden awa'."

c) 1 Thessalonians 4:17—We will be "caught up to meet the Lord in the air." And he concluded: "There's maself awa'."

4
Psalm 41
The Psalm of the Betrayal

PSALM 41

To the chief Musician. A Psalm of David.

1 Blessed is he that considereth the poor: the LORD will deliver him
in time of trouble.
2 The LORD will preserve him, and keep him alive; and he shall be
blessed upon the earth: and Thou wilt not deliver him unto the will
of his enemies.
3 The LORD will strengthen him upon the bed of languishing: Thou
wilt make all his bed in his sickness.
4 I said, LORD, be merciful unto me: heal my soul; for I have sinned
against Thee.
5 Mine enemies speak evil of me, When shall he die, and his name
perish?
6 And if he come to see me, he speaketh vanity: his heart gathereth
iniquity to itself; when he goeth abroad, he telleth it.
7 All that hate me whisper together against me: against me do they
devise my hurt.
8 An evil disease, say they, cleaveth fast unto him: and now that he

lieth he shall rise up no more.
9 Yea, mine own familiar friend, in whom I trusted, which did eat of my bread, hath lifted up his heel against me.
10 But Thou, O LORD, be merciful unto me, and raise me up, that I may requite them.
11 By this I know that Thou favorest me, because mine enemy doth not triumph over me.
12 And as for me, Thou upholdest me in mine integrity, and settest me before Thy face for ever.
13 Blessed be the LORD God of Israel from everlasting, and to everlasting. Amen, and Amen.

THE PSALM OF THE BETRAYAL

The background of Psalm 41 is the rebellion of Absalom against his father, King David, recorded in 2 Samuel 11-16. This is the last of a group of psalms (38-41) which belongs to that period. The last verse of Psalm 41 is the formal conclusion of Book One of the Psalter. The book opens with the Blessed Man of Psalm 1 and closes with the Betrayed Man of Psalm 41.

Psalm 41 is an example of a psalm in which only one verse is definitely Messianic. Verse 9 was quoted by our Lord in John 13:18-19 and applied to Judas Iscariot. The rest of the psalm is David's experience, when some of his best friends, including his own son, conspired against him, and raised an army to overthrow his throne and his kingdom.

These were sufferings which David had brought upon himself as a result of his great sin recorded in 2 Samuel 11. When the prophet Nathan came to David and, after telling the story of the little ewe lamb, dramatically accused him of the sin of adultery and murder, David confessed his sin and truly repented in the words of Psalms 51 and 32. Nathan's reply was: David, your sin is forgiven, but the sword will never depart from your house! David had wrecked a man's home and taken that man's life. He had to reap with bitter tears and suffering what he had done, in the actions of his own sons and family. He had to learn that whatever a man sows, that he also reaps. He had overindulged his handsome and proud son, Absalom; he had shut his eyes and ears to his crimes; now he had to reap the consequences.

Among the conspirators in the Absalom rebellion was Ahithophel, formerly one of David's best friends and a trusted counselor. When David heard that Ahithophel had joined the conspirators, he groaned: "O Lord, I pray Thee, turn the counsel of Ahithophel into foolishness!" (2 Sam. 15:31). His best friend had turned traitor!

When we consider that Ahithophel was grandfather of Bathsheba, we can understand the motive behind his treachery. This is the background to verse 9 of the psalm: "Yea, mine own familiar friend, in whom I trusted, which did eat of my bread, hath lifted up his heel against me." These are the words which our Lord applied to Judas Iscariot and his act of betrayal. Judas would receive the morsel of bread from the hand of the One who was the Bread of Life, and perish still.

There are three other passages in the Old Testament which speak prophetically of the betrayer:

Psalm 69:25 is quoted by Peter in Acts 1:20, "Let their habitation be desolate, and let none dwell in their tents."

Psalm 109:8 was also quoted by Peter: "Let his days be few; and let another take his office" (Acts 1:20).

Zechariah 11:12-13 is the third: "And I said unto them, If ye think good, give me my price; and if not, forbear. So they weighed for my price: thirty pieces of silver. And the Lord said unto me, Cast it unto the potter: a goodly price that I was prized at of them. And I took the thirty pieces of silver, and cast [it unto] the potter in the house of the Lord." This passage is quoted in Matthew 27:9-10.

AN OUTLINE OF PSALM 41

The psalm is in five parts or stanzas:
1. David's confidence in God (vv. 1-3).
2. David confesses his sin (v. 4).
3. The conspirators' whispering campaign (vv. 5-8).
4. His counselor Ahithophel's betrayal (v. 9).
5. David's cry to God for vindication (vv. 10-12).

The psalm, and Book One, ends with the words: "Blessed be the Lord God of Israel from everlasting, and to everlasting. Amen, and Amen."

THE MESSIANIC PASSAGE (V. 9)

The passage is quoted by our Lord in the Upper Room (Jn. 13:18). "He that eateth bread with Me hath lifted up his heel against Me," and is applied to Judas Iscariot. There is a mystery about the person and career of Judas that is difficult to understand, but he is a type of many in the religious world today. His history, as recorded in Scripture, falls into twelve stages or steps.

Judas' mention in prophecy. We have already referred to the four places in the prophetic Word where he appears. His name is not mentioned, but his actions and his end are. It is significant that he has the same name as the man who sold Joseph to the Ishmaelites for twenty pieces of silver (Gen. 37:26-27).

Chosen by the Lord as an apostle. After a whole night spent in prayer, our Lord chose the apostles (Lk. 6:16). He called whom He would, to be with Him, and sent them forth to preach (Mk. 3:13-19). Judas was linked with Simon the Canaanite in this service (Mt. 10:4). He is always last in the list, and always called the traitor or betrayer. He was chosen by the Lord, and yet John 6:64 tells us: "Jesus knew from the beginning who they were that believed not, and who should betray Him." Here we have at the same time the omniscience and the love of the Saviour.

Man is a freewill agent, and not a machine subject to inexorable fate. There came a point in Judas' life when he deliberately chose his own way, in spite of all the love and privilege conferred upon him. He is a type of Christendom's unconverted preachers. "Many will say to Me in that day, Lord, Lord, have we not prophesied in Thy name? and in Thy name have cast out demons? and in Thy name done many wonderful works? And then will I profess unto them, I never knew you: depart from Me ye that work iniquity" (Mt. 7:22-23).

Treasurer of the apostolic band, but a thief (John 12:6). Apparently our Lord, during His public ministry, lived by faith and trust in God for daily needs. We read of "certain women, which had been healed of evil spirits and infirmities, Mary called Magdalene, out of whom went seven devils, and Joanna the wife of Chuza, Herod's steward, and Susanna, and many others, which ministered to Him of their substance" (Lk. 8:2-3). When He sent the apostles on their preaching tours, He instructed them, "Provide neither gold, nor silver, nor brass in your purses, nor scrip for your journey…for the workman is worthy of his meat" (Mt. 10:9-10).

But Judas, as the trusted financial expert of the group, carried the bag and surreptitiously helped himself from their meager resources! How often has the story been repeated in modern times. Sympathetic saints, sometimes out of deep poverty, contribute to worthy causes, and later it is found that the funds have been embezzled by someone in a position of trust. Judas was guilty of this crime.

The anointing of our Lord by Mary of Bethany. Matthew 26 and John 12 record a feast early in Passover week, in which the characters of Mary and Judas respectively are revealed. It was definitely the crisis in the life of Judas. Mary pours the contents of her alabaster flask of precious ointment on the head and feet of Jesus, and wipes His feet with her hair. Mary's act of love and devotion reveals the character of Judas. Note his reaction:

a) His attitude to the Lord: Why this waste? Why was not the ointment sold for three hundred pence and given to the poor? Worship was a foreign idea to him.

b) His attitude to the woman: He instigated indignation and murmuring against her (Mk. 14:4), speaking evil of her good.

c) His attitude to money: He was a thief! He had a gift for evaluation and statistics. But it was not the evaluation of the Holy Spirit, who declares the ointment to be "very precious." Judas' estimate was three hundred pence. Both Matthew and Mark link the anointing and his frustration with his going to the priests to sell the Saviour. "What will you give me?" They agreed on thirty pieces of silver, the price of a slave gored by an ox (Ex. 21:32). It is called in Matthew 27:6 and Acts 1:19 the price of blood. This is the sin of Balaam, Gehazi, Ananias and Sapphira (2 Pet. 2:15; Jn. 13:2; Lk. 22:3; Acts 5:1-11). It has often been said that "a man's attitude to money is an acid test of his character." It was so with Judas Iscariot. From this point on, he sought opportunity to betray the Lord.

At the table (John 13). There are six references to Judas as the apostles sat at the Passover table in the Upper Room. "The devil having now put into the heart of Judas Iscariot, Simon's son, to betray Him" (v. 2). "Ye are clean, but not all. For He knew who should betray Him" (vv. 10-11). The quotation from Psalm 41:9, "He that eateth bread with Me hath lifted up his heel against Me" (v. 18). The outright statement (v. 21), "One of you shall betray Me." The sop (v. 27) consisted of a portion of the passover lamb, the unleavened bread, and the bitter herbs. It was usually offered to an honored guest as a token of courtesy and affection. It was one of the last stabs at the man's conscience. Having received the sop, he went immediately out: and it was night (v. 30). That was a night never to have a sunrise for the betrayer!

Satan enters him. "After the sop, Satan entered into him." Our Lord had previously said (Jn. 6:70-71), "Have not I chosen you twelve, and one of you is a devil *[diabolus]*?" Whenever the word "devil" is applied to an evil spirit, it is always a mistranslation, and ought to be rendered "demon." Our Lord called Judas Iscariot a devil. Satan has many servants at his beck and call to do his infernal work, but when it came to the betrayal of the Saviour, he did not delegate that task to a demon. He himself entered into Judas, and from that point on, Judas was a Satan-possessed man.

At the beginning of our Lord's life, Satan in the person of Herod sought to destroy Him; at the temptation in the wilderness, he tried to move Him out of the position of dependence on His Father's will. Now, at the end, he personally enters into a man to treacherously betray the Son of God's love and purpose.

The arrest in the garden. "Judas...knew the place, for Jesus oft times resorted thither with His disciples" (Jn. 18:1-2). It was a place of retreat and of prayer. The arresting party came with lanterns, torches, and weapons. The identifying sign was a kiss and a salutation. One's mind immediately goes back to Absalom (2 Sam. 15:5-6), who also gave the traitor's kiss. Note that Judas never called Jesus, "Lord." Here it is, "Master, master" (Mk. 14:43-45). Our Lord's reply was, "Friend" *(hetairos,* comrade), one of the most touching entreaties in the Bible (Mt. 26:50).

Judas' return to the Temple (Mt. 27:3-10). When he saw that Jesus was condemned, Judas "repented himself." He probably never expected that Jesus would be condemned and executed. He knew His sinless character and had seen Him a number of times escape from His enemies, but he never counted on this. When the awful truth that Jesus was really going to die dawned on Judas' consciousness, he was filled with remorse. It was not repentance in the real sense of the term. He could not now change his mind, or that of the priests, his co-conspirators. He cried: "I have sinned in that I have betrayed the innocent blood." The priests callously replied: "What is that to us? See thou to that." That is the world's cynical answer to the tortured mind of the criminal. The silver coins burned like fire in Judas' hand; he flung them into the Temple and went out and hanged himself.

The suicide. There are a number of comparisons between Judas and Ahithophel. Both had been in a position of trust and intimacy; both had been treated with kindness and courtesy; both performed an act of treachery; the motive behind Ahithophel's action was probably malice and vengeance, that behind Judas' was greed. Then both committed suicide by hanging.

Our Lord did not quote all of Psalm 41:9. He did not say of Judas that he was one in whom He trusted. He knew him from the beginning and did not commit Himself to him (Jn. 2:24-25). Self-murder is a pathetic act. Its history, not only in Scripture but in the secular records, makes sad reading. Human life is sacred, and its termination should be left in God's hand where it belongs.

The potter's field. Apparently Judas had in mind to buy this piece of real estate. When he was foiled in his purpose by Mary's act of devotion, and his plan on how to use the thirty pieces of silver did not work out, like a moth drawn to the light of a candle, he went to the spot on which his mind had been set, and there took his own life. Peter gives the details in Acts 1:18-20. "Now this man purchased a field with the reward of iniquity; and falling headlong, he burst asunder in the midst, and all his bowels gushed out. And it was known to all the dwellers at Jerusalem; insomuch as that field is called in their proper tongue, Aceldama, that is to say, The field of blood." It is possible, in attempting to hang himself, the rope broke, with the result that Peter describes.

Matthias takes his place (Acts 1:20-26). Because Matthias is never mentioned again in Scripture, some say that Peter acted in a hurry, and that Paul was the man chosen by God to take the place of Judas as an apostle. But Paul's apostleship was unique. Peter gives us the qualifications of the man chosen to take the place of Judas and to be numbered among the twelve. "Wherefore of these men which have companied with us all the time that the Lord Jesus went in and out among us, beginning from the baptism of John, unto that same day that He was taken up from us, must one be ordained to be a witness with us of His resurrection." We have to take the record as it stands, that Matthias was God's choice.

Judas went to his own place. Our Lord told Simon Peter that He was going to prepare a place in the Father's house (Jn. 14:1-3). But here is another place prepared for the son of perdition. The term "son of perdition" is used again only of the man of sin (2 Thess. 2:3). He, too, will ultimately find himself in the same place. It is a place of: *distance*—Judas was near to the Lord on earth, but now a great gulf is fixed (Lk. 16:26); *darkness*—he went out into the night, ultimately the outer darkness (Mt. 25:30); *defilement—for* he that is filthy, let him be filthy still (Rev. 22:11); and it is a place of *despair*—for such punishment is everlasting; in that place there is no hope (Mt. 25:46).

There are ultimately only two places—heaven and hell. Where do you have your place?

5
Psalm 22
The Psalm of the Crucifixion

PSALM 22

To the chief Musician upon Aijeleth Shahar.
A Psalm of David.

1 My God, My God, why hast Thou forsaken Me? why art Thou so
far from helping Me, and from the words of My roaring?
2 O My God, I cry in the daytime, but Thou hearest not; and in the
night season, and am not silent.
3 But Thou art holy, O Thou that inhabitest the praises of Israel.
4 Our fathers trusted in Thee: they trusted, and Thou didst deliver
them.
5 They cried unto Thee, and were delivered: they trusted in Thee,
and were not confounded.
6 But I am a worm, and no man; a reproach of men, and despised of
the people.
7 All they that see Me laugh Me to scorn: they shoot out the lip, they
shake the head, saying,
8 He trusted on the LORD that He would deliver Him: let Him de-

liver Him, seeing He delighted in Him.
9 But Thou art He that took Me out of the womb: Thou didst make
Me hope when I was upon My mother's breasts.
10 I was cast upon Thee from the womb: Thou art My God from My
mother's belly.
11 Be not far from Me; for trouble is near; for there is none to help.
12 Many bulls have compassed Me: strong bulls of Bashan have
beset Me round.
13 They gaped upon Me with their mouths, as a ravening and a roar-
ing lion.
14 1 am poured out like water, and all My bones are out of joint: My
heart is like wax; it is melted in the midst of My bowels.
15 My strength is dried up like a potsherd; and My tongue cleaveth
to My jaws; and Thou hast brought Me into the dust of death.
16 For dogs have compassed Me: the assembly of the wicked have
inclosed Me: they pierced My hands and My feet.
17 I may tell all My bones: they look and stare upon Me.
18 They part My garments among them, and cast lots upon My ves-
ture.
19 But be not Thou far from Me, O LORD: O My strength, haste
Thee to help Me.
20 Deliver My soul from the sword; My darling from the power of
the dog.
21 Save Me from the lion's mouth: for Thou hast heard Me from the
horns of the unicorns.
22 I will declare Thy name unto My brethren: in the midst of the
congregation will I praise Thee.
23 Ye that fear the LORD, praise Him; all ye the seed of Jacob, glori-
fy Him; and fear Him, all ye the seed of Israel.
24 For He hath not despised nor abhorred the affliction of the afflict-
ed; neither hath He hid His face from Him; but when He cried unto
Him, He heard.
25 My praise shall be of Thee in the great congregation: I will pay
My vows before them that fear Him.
26 The meek shall eat and be satisfied: they shall praise the LORD

that seek Him: your heart shall live for ever.
27 All the ends of the world shall remember and turn unto the
LORD: and all the kindreds of the nations shall worship before Thee.
28 For the kingdom is the LORD'S: and He is the governor among
the nations.
29 All they that be fat upon earth shall eat and worship: all they that
go down to the dust shall bow before Him: and none can keep alive
his own soul.
30 A seed shall serve Him; it shall be accounted to the Lord for a
generation.
31 They shall come, and shall declare His righteousness unto a peo-
ple that shall be born, that He hath done this.

THE PSALM OF THE CRUCIFIXION

There are four psalms that speak of the death of Christ, each looking at it from a different standpoint:

Psalm 40 is the burnt offering—revealing God's purpose.
Psalm 22 is the sin offering—describing the passion.
Psalm 69 is the trespass offering—and the penalty.
Psalm 118 is the peace offering—the prophetic program.

Perhaps the most important is Psalm 22 on account of the wealth of detail and the universal results that issue from the sacrificial death of Christ on the cross. This goes wider and deeper than the others.

The psalm was written by David circa BC 1050. It contains thirty-three items describing death by crucifixion. When we consider that this cruel and painful method of execution was invented many centuries later, it gives us a vivid demonstration of the inspiration of Holy Scripture by the Spirit of God.

The psalm divides into two parts. The dividing point comes in the center of verse 21, where the suffering Saviour cries, "Thou hast heard Me!" Everything previous to this is suffering; everything after it is an unbroken song.

AN OUTLINE OF PSALM 22

Each part has three sections:

1. Suffering from a threefold source:
   a) Divinely from God (vv. 1-6a)—the holiness of God.
   b) physically from man (vv. 6b-18)—hatred of man.
   c) diabolically from Satan (vv. 19-21a)—his hostility.
2. The second section reveals three circles of blessing in resurrection (vv. 21b-31):
   a) My brethren (v. 22).
   b) Seed of Jacob, seed of Israel (v. 23).
   c) All the ends of the world (v. 27).

Two banquet tables are spread in the psalm: The meek shall eat and be satisfied (v. 26); and all they that be fat upon earth shall eat and worship (v. 29).

To the chief musician upon Aijeleth Shahar. The Hebrew words of the title mean: "The hind of the dawn." The ancient synagogue took the title as a name for the Shekinah, and as a symbol of dawning redemption, and applied it to the morning sacrifice.

Delitzsch says that, according to the traditional definition, it refers to "the early light preceding the dawn of the morning, whose first rays are likened to the horns of a hind." And the kibbutz Aiyalet ha-Shahar in Galilee today has the figure of a hind leaping over the rising sun at its entryway.

Because the hart and the hind (male and female deer) are often referred to in the poetical books and applied symbolically to our Lord, could it not be applied also in this psalm? (see Song of Sol. 2:17; 8:14). The psalm mentions a number of animals that are the enemies of the "hind of the dawn" and that bring it down into the dust of death. In that case, a key to the interpretation of the psalm hangs at the door.

FOUR APPLICATIONS OF PSALM 22

1. *Symbolic:* the hind of the dawn and its enemies.

2. *Messianic:* notice especially four remarkable titles—the worm, My darling, the leader of praise, and the Governor among the nations.

3. *Historic:* it describes the birth, death, resurrection, exaltation of the Messiah.

4. *Prophetic:* there are three circles of blessing, ending with the kingdom.

1. THE SYMBOLIC: THE HIND OF THE DAWN AND ITS ENEMIES

In the Mosaic economy, our Lord as the sinless sacrifice is typified by the ox (*son of the herd*), the ram, the lamb, the kid, and the turtle dove. These were slain and offered on the altar. But in the poetical books, He is compared to the hind of the dawn, which is generally seen in the early morning, tripping along in the forest glades, licking the dew, and taking a bite of the succulent leaves as it makes its way along. It is one of the most beautiful creatures that God has made, but it is also defenseless. Its only means of survival are a keen sense of smell and speed in flight. It has many enemies in an environment where nature, "red in tooth and claw," reigns supreme. This is the beautiful figure used of our Lord in Psalm 22. Four of its enemies are mentioned:

The bulls of Bashan (v. 12). The Prophet Amos (4:1) compares the leaders of the nation to the cattle of Bashan, and castigates them for oppressing the poor and crushing the needy. These are the ceremonially clean bulls, the highest of the offerings in Jerusalem. They would correspond to the chief priests and scribes who were responsible for the arrest and illegal trial of Christ, and who handed Him over to Pilate and the Roman government for execution. They cried: "His blood be on us and on our children" (Mt. 27:25), and there it remains until the present day. It will only be removed when, in a coming day, at His appearing, they will look on Him whom they pierced, and in true repentance they will confess their sin, and a fountain will be opened for sin and for uncleanness (Zech. 12:10-13:1).

The unicorn or wild ox (Hebrew, *reem)* (v. 21). H. A. Ironside writes: "There is no such animal as a unicorn. Our translators put that word in because they did not understand the exact meaning, but every Hebrew scholar now knows that it is the aurochs, a wild ox with great branching horns, as sharp almost as needles at the ends. The executioners used to lay hold of poor, wretched, condemned victims, bind them by the feet and the shoulders on these sharp horns, and then set the wild ox loose in the desert to run about until the man died. That is the picture used here. Crucifixion was like putting the man upon the horns of the wild ox."

The word could also refer to the wild buffalo. It is one of the most powerful, vicious, malevolent beasts in the African forest, especially when aroused or wounded. It will pound its victim to pulp with its massive head and horns. It could be compared to the mob outside Pilate's courtroom, howling in unison: "Away with Him, away with Him, crucify Him!" (Jn. 19:15). There are few things more frightening or vicious than a mob out of control.

The dog. The dog is mentioned twice, first in the plural (v. 16). "For dogs have compassed Me: the assembly of the wicked have inclosed Me: they pierced My hands and My feet." This could refer to the Roman soldiers who carried out the execution. Then (v. 20): "Deliver My soul from the sword; My darling from the power of the dog." This could be applied to Pilate, who in spite of his own statement, "I find no fault in Him," sent Him to the death of the cross. He was the official representative of the power and authority of Rome. The dog in Scripture usually refers to the Gentile, the pariah dog. "How perfectly man was revealed in the presence of the cross! The dogs, heartless, shameless, unclean, and offal-feeding, hunting in packs like the assembly of the evil-doers here" (F. W. Grant).

The lion. Satan is called a roaring lion (1 Pet. 5:8). While amid the darkness, God had forsaken His well-beloved, and angelic help was absent, Satan and his hosts were there. Satan, after the temptation in the wilderness, left Him for a season. But he came back to the attack. He entered personally into Judas to do his nefarious work (Jn. 13:27). But it was on the cross that the final attack was made.

There is an important passage (Col. 2:14-15) which shows that, as well as Satan, the hosts of hell joined in the attack on Christ on the cross: "And having spoiled principalities and powers, He made a show of them openly, triumphing over them in it." The horns of the wild ox, the paw of the dog, and the lion's mouth are dangerous weapons, but it was none of these that brought the Hind of the Dawn down into the dust of death. He was superior to them all.

The sword (v. 20). The sword of divine justice was sheathed in the bosom of the Good Shepherd. "Awake, O sword, against My shepherd, and against the man that is My fellow, saith the Lord of hosts: smite the shepherd, and the sheep shall be scattered: and I will turn Mine hand upon the little ones" (Zech. 13:7).

Jehovah bade His sword awake;
O Christ, it woke 'gainst Thee.
Thy blood its flaming blade must slake:
Thy heart its sheath must be.
All for my sake, my peace to make,
Now sleeps that sword for me! —*Ann Ross Cousin*

It is worth noting that the Hebrew word for dust (v. 15), "Thou hast brought Me into the dust of death," is *aphar.* It is usually translated "dust," but in Numbers 19:17 it is translated "ashes." There it refers to the ashes of the burnt red heifer which were used for the ceremonial purification of sin.

2. FOUR MESSIANIC TITLES

I am a worm (v. 6—Hebrew, *tolaath).* The word occurs 31 times in the Old Testament and is often translated "scarlet" or "crimson." "The word applies especially to the coccus from which the scarlet dye of the Tabernacle was obtained, of course by its death...Indeed the word is used in Isaiah 1:18 for the color of sin, and that of a heinous kind" (F. W. Grant).

"The *tola* of the Orient is a little worm, something like the cochineal of Mexico, which feeds on a certain kind of cactus. The people beat these plants until the cochineal fall into a basin and then they crush those little insects. The blood is that brilliant crimson dye that makes those bright Mexican garments. In Palestine and Syria, they use the *tola* in the same way and it makes the beautiful permanent scarlet dye of the Orient. It was very expensive and was worn only by the rich and the noble. It is referred to again and again in Scripture. Solomon is said to have clothed the maidens of Israel in scarlet. Daniel was to be clothed in scarlet by Belshazzar. And that word 'scarlet' is literally 'the splendor of a worm.' Now the Lord Jesus Christ says, 'I am a worm; I am the *tola,'* and He had to be crushed in death that you and I might be clothed in glory. The glorious garments of our salvation are the garments that have been procured as a result of His death and suffering" (H. A. Ironside).

The title "worm" would remind us of His humiliation at the hands of man. To the title He adds, "and no man" *(lo-ish).* Not "no man" in the sense of not being a man; but a nobody in contrast to being a somebody. When a well-known evangelical preacher gave out the hymn, "Would He devote that sacred head for such a worm as I?" the choir leader objected, saying, "I refuse to consider myself a worm!" The preacher replied, "My dear brother, a greater One than you or I took that title for Himself!"

My Darling (v. 20). Newberry translates this, "My only-one," as do also the Revised Version and Young. The Septuagint has *monogenes,* the only-begotten, used five times by the Apostle John. It is also used of Isaac in Genesis 22:2. The Lord Jesus is the unique, only-begotten Son in His essential deity, and the first begotten from the dead in His resurrection. So if the worm speaks of His humiliation and His humanity, My only-One emphasizes His dignity and deity.

The Leader of Praise (v. 22). "I will declare Thy name unto My brethren: in the midst of the congregation will I praise Thee." This is clearly the language of resurrection. "Go to My brethren," He said to Mary Magdalene on Resurrection Day, "and say unto them, I ascend unto My Father, and your Father; and to My God, and your God." Here He declares the Name. The next clause, "in the midst of the congregation will I praise Thee," is quoted in Hebrews 2:12, where the word "congregation" is changed to "church." Not only is He the Leader and the object of praise among His people today, but it points forward to that great symphony of praise and worship described in Revelation 5, when the Lamb in the midst of the throne will be worshiped and adored.

The Governor among the Nations (v. 28). The latter part of the psalm speaks of millennial days when the government will be upon His shoulder; He shall reign from sea to sea and from the river to the ends of the earth. Then and only then will righteousness reign, and for the first time this poor suffering world will have a government free from corruption and oppression. Our hearts cry, "Come, Lord Jesus!"

3. THE HISTORIC INTERPRETATION

Max Isaac Reich, the Hebrew Christian and commentator, points out that there are 33 prophecies in this psalm, all fulfilled at the cross. It is indeed tragic that Israel is still blind to its message. Chapter 53 of Isaiah is omitted in the Sabbath readings in the synagogue. So this psalm is also avoided. Professor Claude Montefiore's commentary on the Psalms deals with Psalms 21 and 23, but omits any reference to Psalm 22. It is to Jewish unbelief "a stone of stumbling and a rock of offense."

The psalm begins and ends with two cries of Christ on the cross: "My God, My God, why hast Thou forsaken Me?" (v. 1), and "that He hath done this [it is finished] " (v. 31).

His birth is indicated by four statements (vv. 9-10): "But Thou art He that took Me out of the womb: Thou didst make Me hope when I was upon My mother's breasts: I was cast upon Thee from the womb: Thou art My God from My mother's belly."

His rejection by Israel is indicated in verses 6-8. He is "a reproach of men, and despised of the people. All they that see Me laugh Me to scorn; they shoot out the lip, they shake the head saying, He trusted on the Lord that He would deliver Him, let Him deliver Him, seeing He delighted in Him."

Between "Immanuel's orphan cry" in verse 1 and His triumphant cry of victory in verse 31, there are five distinct items of Calvary's shame.

a) Alternating periods of light and darkness in verse 2 (Mt. 27:45-46).

b) Mockery (v. 8). The exact words are recorded in Matthew 27:43.

c) The disrobing prior to the crucifixion (v. 18) was fulfilled in minute detail, even to the gambling for the seamless robe (Jn. 19:24).

d) The pierced hands and feet (v. 16). The NEB gives the horrible translation, "They hacked off My hands and My feet." This shows a distinct bias against the Messianic interpretation of the psalm. Certainly this was never true of David, the author of the psalm, or of anyone recorded in history. But our blessed Lord's hands and feet were pierced and also His side riven (Jn. 19:37).

e) His thirst (vv. 14-15) was mentioned again in Psalm 69:21 and literally fulfilled (Jn. 19:28-30).

His resurrection is indicated in verse 21b, in His victorious cry: "Thou hast heard Me!" (See Hebrews 5:7). He was saved, not from death, but out of death. Hallelujah! He arose!

4. THE PROPHETIC APPLICATION

From verse 22 to the end, the horizon gradually widens until at last all the ends of the world shall remember and turn to the Lord (v. 27):

a) First is the congregation, translated by the word "church" in Hebrews 2:12, where the words are quoted and applied to believers of the present dispensation. We are His brethren, sharers of His joy and of all the blessings which come from His sacrificial death on the cross.

b) Secondly, the seed of Jacob and the seed of Israel (v. 23) are mentioned. The Jew today, in unbelief and in the Lo-ammi ("not a people"—Hos. 1:9) position, will one day be restored and brought back into covenant relationship with Jehovah. They will look on Him whom they pierced, and one day will be the olive tree, bringing forth fruit for God.

c) Finally, "all the ends of the world shall remember and turn unto the Lord" (v. 27). "For the kingdom is the Lord's" (v. 28).

The blessings of Calvary cannot be confined to the Church alone or to the Jew. The ever-widening power of these blessings will eventually result in the establishment of the kingdom. The rejected Man of Calvary will one day be King of kings and Lord of lords! "And there were great voices in heaven, saying, The kingdoms of this world are become the kingdoms of our Lord, and of His Christ; and He shall reign for ever and ever" (Rev. 11:15).

In that day there will be universal praise and worship.

There will also be universal plenty. "All they that be fat upon earth shall eat and worship" (v. 29). The cross will be the source of material blessing as well as meeting the spiritual needs of all who look in faith to the One who died thereon.

The psalm concludes with a spiritual seed and each succeeding generation hearing the glorious message of the cross, "that He hath done this," that *It is finished.*

6
Psalm 69
The Psalm of the Trespass Offering

PSALM 69

To the chief Musician upon Shoshannim
A Psalm of David

1 Save me, O God; for the waters are come in unto my soul.
2 I sink in deep mire, where there is no standing: I am come into
deep waters, where the floods overflow me.
3 1 am weary of my crying: my throat is dried: mine eyes fail while I
wait for my God.
4 They that hate me without a cause are more than the hairs of mine
head: they that would destroy me, being mine enemies wrongfully,
are mighty: then I restored that which I took not away.
5 O God, Thou knowest my foolishness; and my sins are not hid
from Thee.
6 Let not them that wait on Thee, O Lord GOD of hosts, be ashamed
for my sake: let not those that seek Thee be confounded for my sake,
O God of Israel.
7 Because for Thy sake I have borne reproach; shame hath covered

my face.
8 I am become a stranger unto my brethren, and an alien unto my mother's children.
9 For the zeal of Thine house hath eaten me up; and the reproaches of them that reproached Thee are fallen upon me.
10 When I wept, and chastened my soul with fasting, that was to my reproach.
11 I made sackcloth also my garment; and I became a proverb to them.
12 They that sit in the gate speak against me; and I was the song of the drunkards.
13 But as for me, my prayer is unto Thee, O LORD, in an acceptable time: O God, in the multitude of Thy mercy hear me, in the truth of Thy salvation.
14 Deliver me out of the mire, and let me not sink: let me be delivered from them that hate me, and out of the deep waters.
15 Let not the waterflood overflow me, neither let the deep swallow me up, and let not the pit shut her mouth upon me.
16 Hear me, O LORD; for Thy lovingkindness is good: turn unto me according to the multitude of Thy tender mercies.
17 And hide not Thy face from Thy servant; for I am in trouble: hear me speedily.
18 Draw nigh unto my soul, and redeem it: deliver me because of mine enemies.
19 Thou hast known my reproach, and my shame, and my dishonor: mine adversaries are all before Thee.
20 Reproach hath broken my heart; and I am full of heaviness: and I looked for some to take pity, but there was none; and for comforters, but I found none.
21 They gave me also gall for my meat; and in my thirst they gave me vinegar to drink.
22 Let their table become a snare before them: and that which should have been for their welfare, let it become a trap.
23 Let their eyes be darkened, that they see not; and make their loins continually to shake.

24 Pour out Thine indignation upon them, and let Thy wrathful anger take hold of them.
25 Let their habitation be desolate; and let none dwell in their tents.
26 For they persecute him whom Thou hast smitten; and they talk to the grief of those whom Thou hast wounded.
27 Add iniquity unto their iniquity: and let them not come into Thy righteousness.
28 Let them be blotted out of the book of the living, and not be written with the righteous.
29 But I am poor and sorrowful: let Thy salvation, O God, set me up on high.
30 I will praise the name of Cod with a song, and will magnify Him with thanksgiving.
31 This also shall please the LORD better than an ox or bullock that hath horns and hoofs.
32 The humble shall see this, and be glad: and your heart shall live that seek God.
33 For the LORD heareth the poor, and despiseth not his prisoners.
34 Let the heaven and earth praise Him, the seas, and every thing that moveth therein.
35 For God will save Zion, and will build the cities of Judah: that they may dwell there, and have it in possession.
36 The seed also of His servants shall inherit it: and they that love His name shall dwell therein.

THE PSALM OF THE TRESPASS OFFERING

There are seven quotations from Psalm 69 in the New Testament referring to the Messiah, so we are on safe ground in calling it a Messianic psalm. The key word is in verse 4. "Then I restored that which I took not away." He paid the price and suffered the penalty for sin. He added the fifth part, making reparation for the sins of the world. His sacrificial death was the fulfillment of the guilt offering (Lev. 5:1-6:7).

To the chief musician upon Shoshannim. A Psalm of David. The word *shoshannim* in the title means lilies. They often grow in the mire and mud (v. 2). The four psalms that have this title were traditionally associated with springtime and the passover season. A writer in Israel describes the lily as luxuriating in the valleys and usually growing among thorns. Nothing can be in higher contrast than the beautiful velvety softness of the lily and the crabbed tangled mass of thorns. It speaks of the purity of our Lord in a world where the thorns of the curse abound. On the cross they put a crown of thorns on His head. In contrast, we have the lily with its perfect form, spotless purity, vivid color, and fragrant odor. In the Song of Solomon the lily indicates what the Lord thinks of His people, but in the psalms, what they think of Him.

In Scripture the lily is found in four places, corresponding to the four psalms where we find the title:

a) The lily of the valley—the low place at the cross (Ps. 69).

b) The lily of the field—the king in all his glory (Mt. 6:28; Ps. 45).

c) The lily among thorns—trial and tribulation (Ps. 80).

d) The lily in the garden—testimony and victory (Ps. 60).

The Septuagint version renders *shoshannim* as "those that shall be changed through seeing the immortal loveliness of the resurrection."

AN OUTLINE OF PSALM 69

The psalm falls into five parts:

1. The Sufferer and His sorrow (vv. 1-12).
2. The sanctuary-refuge. From weeping, He turns to praying (vv. 13-18).
3. The cross—the broken heart (vv. 19-21).
4. Imprecation—Judas and the nation (vv. 22-28).
5. The song and the seed (vv. 29-36).

1. THE SUFFERER AND HIS SORROW (VV. 1-12)

The Sufferer speaks of the deep mire, black, filthy, vile, the diver's dread; the deep waters, the overwhelming flood; and finally the pit (v. 15). The tomb shuts its mouth. Here we have the deep mystery of God's judgment on sin.

Whatever may have been David's experience, the words have their final fulfillment in the suffering Saviour on Calvary's cross. In Psalm 22, He cried: "Save Me from the lion's mouth," but here it is, "Save Me, O God; for the waters are come in unto My soul." We know that that cry was heard in resurrection in both Psalm 22 and Psalm 69.

There are three main reasons for His sorrow:

1. *Rejection.* First, by the nation (v. 4). He was hated without a cause (Jn. 15:25). Secondly, He was rejected by His family (v. 8; Jn. 7:3-5). Thirdly, He was rebuffed in the Temple, His Father's house (v. 9; Jn. 2:17). Finally, He became an outcast by society (v. 12). By the highest in the land—the judge in the gate, and by the lowest—for He was the song of the drunkard, our Saviour was rejected by those He came to save.

2. *Reproach.* The term is mentioned six times and is one of the key words of the psalm. Reproach is a mixture of contempt, slander, and mockery.

3. *Reparation.* In spite of such treatment, He carried on His course: "Then I restored that which I took not away" (v. 4).

THE TRESPASS OFFERING

He did not take away our innocence, our fellowship with God, nor the dominion which was committed to man before the fall. But in His great work of redemption, reconciliation, and restitution, He has restored all that Adam lost at the Fall—and infinitely more.

Sin is the most costly thing in the universe. Only the precious blood of Christ is of greater value. To understand the havoc that sin has wrought, we must explore three great oceans: the ocean of human suffering since the Fall; the fathomless ocean of the suffering of the Saviour on the cross; and the eternal suffering of the lost in hell and the lake of fire.

We notice as well that, in the trespass offering, there are three injured parties: the holy things of the Lord, for God's honor has been insulted; things forbidden in the decalogue, for the Law has been broken; and a neighbor has suffered.

The neighbor has been injured in one or more of five areas:

a) *In things* delivered to keep, and lying concerning it. This could be applied to a person entrusted with funds, who embezzles them.

b) *In fellowship.* A man trusts his brother—a business partner—and has nothing in writing, then gets hurt. He has no redress or comeback.

c) *A thing taken away by violence.* Like Naboth's vineyard, it refers to the man who drives a hard bargain.

d) *The man who deceived his neighbor.* This includes fraudulent bankruptcy or cheating the tax collector.

e) *Finds that which is lost, and lies concerning it.* The trespass offering would be used in cases of robbing the employer of time or tools, of perjury, or of greed for gain, backed by lies.

When the trespass was discovered, then reparation had to be made. Moses, the lawgiver, made the valuation of the loss involved in the crime, and restitution had to be made according to the shekel of the sanctuary.

As well as the actual value of the loss sustained, one-fifth or 20 per cent had to be added. Then a sacrifice had to be offered to God. Not a lamb, but a ram, the leader of the flock (Gen. 22:13). If the crime was against his neighbor, restitution had to be made first, and then the sacrificial offering (Mt. 5:23-24).

APPLICATION OF THE TRESPASS OFFERING TO THE WORK OF CHRIST

The infinite value of the atonement. Propitiation was for the whole world (1 Jn. 2:1-2). John the Baptist, Christ's forerunner, declared: "Behold the Lamb of God which taketh away the sin of the world!" (Jn. 1:29). He gave Himself "a ransom for all," Paul affirms (1 Tim. 2:6). The sacrifice and the value of the precious blood was infinite, *sufficient* for all, but it is only *efficient* to those who believe (Rom. 3:22). The doctrine of a limited atonement is unscriptural. The 20 per cent added in the trespass offering makes this plain.

Reconciliation. This again is threefold. "And having made peace through the blood of His cross, by Him to reconcile all things unto Himself; by Him, I say, whether they be things in earth, or things in heaven. And you, that were sometime alienated and enemies in your mind by wicked works, yet now hath He reconciled in the body of His flesh through death, to present you holy and unblameable and unreproveable in His sight" (Col. 1:20-22).

The Restitution of all things. This anticipates the millennium. The groaning creation will be restored. The Bible's history is not a circle but a spiral. Revelation 22 is higher than Genesis 2. Complete redemption anticipates not just man in innocence, but in perfect conformity to the image of Christ. The image and the likeness restored.

2. THE SANCTUARY-REFUGE: WEEPING TO PRAYING (VV. 13-18)

"But as for me, my prayer is unto Thee, O Lord" (v. 13). "Hear me, O Lord; for Thy lovingkindness is good" (v. 16). He cries to be delivered from the mire, the deep waters, the waterflood, and the pit. Above all, He asks to be delivered from His enemies and those that hate Him.

How this reminds us of the agony and the bloodlike sweat of Gethsemane, of the strong crying and tears unto Him that was able to save Him out of death, and we know that He was heard "in that He feared" (Heb. 5:7).

3. THE CROSS: THE BROKEN HEART (VV. 19-21)

"Thou hast known my reproach and my shame" (v. 19). "Reproach hath broken my heart" (v. 20). "Because for thy sake I have borne reproach" (v. 7). "The reproaches of them that reproached Thee [have] fallen upon me" (v. 9). "When I wept, and chastened my soul with fasting, that was to my reproach" (v. 10). Altogether the word "reproach" occurs six times. It was literally fulfilled in the mockery and insult that was flung at the Son of God when He hung upon the cross.

The Gospels record that our Lord was mocked in a threefold way:

At His trial before the Sanhedrin, He was mocked *as a Prophet.* "And some began to spit on Him, and to cover His face, and to buffet Him, and to say unto Him, Prophesy: and the servants did strike Him with the palms of their hands" (Mk. 14:65).

Before Pilate, He was mocked *as a King.* Twelve times in John's Gospel, Jesus is called the King—at the beginning in worship (Jn. 1:49), but at the end in mockery. Roman soldiers staged a mock coronation ceremony, put on Him a mock royal robe, a crown of thorns on His head, a mock scepter in His hand, and, bowing the knee, said: "Hail, King of the Jews."

On the cross He was mocked *as the Saviour.* Both the malefactors and the people derided Him, saying, "He saved others; let Him save Himself, if He be [the] Christ, the chosen of God."

His reaction to all this was, "Reproach hath broken My heart...I looked for some to take pity, but there was none; and for comforters, but I found none."

His last request before He died was for a refreshing drink.

He cried: "I thirst!" Then verse 21 was fulfilled: "They gave Me also gall for My meat, and in My thirst they gave Me vinegar to drink." Having accomplished all, He cried, "It is finished," and He bowed His head and rendered up His spirit (Jn. 19:30).

4. IMPRECATION: JUDAS AND THE NATION (VV. 22-28)

"These imprecations do not belong to the spirit of the New Testament, and are in sharp contrast to the prayers of Jesus and Stephen, but underlying them is an ethical principle which we cannot afford to ignore. Right is right and wrong is wrong, and God is just" (W. Graham Scroggie).

This passage has to do with the judicial setting aside of the nation of Israel on account of their rejection and crucifixion of their Messiah. This is shown by the language of Romans 11:9-10. They also are applicable to the treacherous betrayal of Christ by Judas Iscariot, as shown by Acts 1:20.

The present age of grace is one in which we are taught to forgive our enemies and pray for those who despitefully use us. But in a coming day, grace will give way to judgment, and loving entreaty, which has been flouted and ignored, to punishment without mercy. God is a God of love, but He is also a God of holiness and righteousness. Sin and rebellion bring their own reward in judgment, just as night follows day.

5. THE SONG AND THE SEED (VV. 29-36)

The conclusion of the psalm parallels the final stanzas of Psalm 22: the Sufferer with His sorrow gives place to a song of praise. The singer in verse 29 prays, "Let Thy salvation, O God, set Me up on high." The answer to the prayer is the resurrection and the ascension. The Lord is the only One of the sons of men to sing on both sides of the sea of death. In the Upper Room, He led the choir of the eleven disciples before

He went out to Gethsemane and the Cross (Mt. 26:30). Here He leads the song on the other side. "I will declare Thy name unto My brethren: in the midst of the congregation will I praise Thee" (Ps. 22:22). This pleases the Lord better than an ox or bullock that has horns and hoofs. The harmony of the song goes out to four groups among men: the humble, those that seek after God, the poor, and the prisoner (vv. 32-33). Then the heavens and earth join in the anthem, the seas and everything that moves therein. Finally it reaches out to Israel, today in unbelief, but one day restored and forgiven.

The Seed in verse 36 is reminiscent of the promise to Abraham. The dust of the earth, the stars of heaven, and the sand of the seashore all remind us of the promise of Genesis 22:17. (Cf., Ps. 22:23,30; Isa. 6:13.)

7
Psalm 16
The Burial, Resurrection & Exaltation of Messiah

PSALM 16

Michtam of David

1 Preserve me, O God: for in Thee do I put my trust.
2 O my soul, thou hast said unto the LORD, Thou art my Lord: my
goodness extendeth not to Thee;
3 But to the saints that are in the earth, and to the excellent, in whom
is all my delight.
4 Their sorrows shall be multiplied that hasten after another god:
their drink-offerings of blood will I not offer, nor take up their
names into my lips.
5 The LORD is the portion of mine inheritance and of my cup: Thou
maintainest my lot.
6 The lines are fallen unto me in pleasant places; yea, I have a goodly
heritage.
7 I will bless the LORD, who hath given me counsel: my reins also
instruct me in the night seasons.

8 I have set the LORD always before me: because He is at my right hand, I shall not be moved.
9 Therefore my heart is glad, and my glory rejoiceth: my flesh also shall rest in hope.
10 For Thou wilt not leave My soul in hell; neither wilt Thou suffer Thine Holy One to see corruption.
11 Thou wilt show me the path of life: in Thy presence is fullness of joy; at Thy right hand there are pleasures for evermore.

BURIAL, RESURRECTION & EXALTATION OF MESSIAH

H. A. Ironside calls Psalm 16 the psalm of the meal offering. It describes the holy, pure life of the Messiah, ending with His exaltation to God's right hand. The typical ingredients of fine flour, oil, salt, and frankincense, and the exclusion of leaven and honey and their meaning were manifested in our Lord's pathway on earth. If in Psalm 1 we see the blessed Man, in Psalm 22 the forsaken Man, in Psalm 16 we see the dependent Man, ending with the risen and exalted Man.

The psalm is quoted by Peter in his Pentecost address (Acts 2:25-28) and by Paul in his address in the synagogue at Antioch in Pisidia, and applied by both to the Lord Jesus, giving us our authority for regarding it as a Messianic psalm (Acts 13:35).

Mitcham of David. There are six psalms that have this title. They all refer to the time of David's rejection. There are several explanations of the term *mitcham.* Some say it is derived from a verb "to engrave."

The Septuagint, in its inscription to the psalm, says: "To be inscribed and hung up on a pillar to commemorate victory." Others translate the title "golden." It has been called "David's golden jewel." Certainly the psalm is a gold mine of teaching concerning our blessed Lord, and the gold of that land is good!

AN OUTLINE OF PSALM 16

The psalm is in two parts:

1. The pathway of faith. Portraying the dependent man, it is beautifully illustrated by the meal offering (vv. 1-7).

2. The pathway of life. The burial, resurrection, and exaltation to God's right hand are previewed (vv. 8-11).

It is helpful to read this psalm in the Revised Version, especially verses 2 and 3.

1. THE PATHWAY OF FAITH OF THE DEPENDENT MAN (VV. 1-7)

The first section presents five attitudes of our Lord in His pilgrim pathway on earth. F. W. Grant suggests it is a divine Pilgrim's Progress. But unlike Bunyan's pilgrim, He is the perfect Pilgrim. There is no bypath meadow!

His attitude to God (vv. 1-2). "Preserve me, O God: for in Thee do I put my trust." The word translated "preserve" in verse 1 does not necessarily mean or imply threatening danger. It is translated "keep" nearly three hundred times in the Old Testament. In the Psalms it is used predominantly for observing God's way, truth, and precepts. It is instructive to notice that God is mentioned sixteen times in the psalm as follows: Jehovah, four times; Thou, Thee, or Thy, nine times; El, Adonai, and He, once each. Thus in nine out of sixteen instances, God is directly addressed, showing that the eyes of the speaker are turned upward towards Him whom he trusts for protection, counsel, and guidance.

This attitude of dependence upon, and subjection to, the will of His Father was a voluntary position which our Lord took in incarnation. He never acted independently. This was the manner in which sin was introduced to mankind in Eden. Eve acted independently of her head, Adam, and the language of anarchy and rebellion ever since has been: "I will do what I like, I will go where I like, and it is nobody's business but my own." This was the essence of the temptation of Christ by Satan in the wilderness at the commencement of His public ministry. Satan attempted to get Him to act independently of the will of His Father. But where our first parents fell, He, as the last Adam, gloriously overcame. In verse 2, He exclaims: "O My soul, Thou hast said to Jehovah, Thou art My Adonai [Sovereign Lord or Master], I have no good beyond Thee!" (see RV). God was the boundary line of His horizon.

His attitude to the people of God (v. 3). "As for the saints that are in the earth, They are the excellent in whom is all My delight." The word "excellent" means "nobles, persons of moral excellence." The title, "His Excellency," more properly belongs to the meanest saint than to the highest governor. They are the aristocracy of Heaven, the highest nobility, the right honorables. Spurgeon has said that Stars and Garters are poor distinctions compared with the graces of the Spirit.

In Malachi's day there was such a company of "saints" and "nobles." They were called "God's peculiar treasure." A similar company existed when our Lord came to earth. There were His parents, humble people of the house of David. The loyal band also included John the Baptist, the fishermen apostles, the Bethany family, and the women who ministered to Him. Note what Moses thought of the people of God. When he was sorely tried, he called them "rebels" (Num. 20:10). But when he was about to leave them, he wrote: "Who is like unto thee, a people saved by the Lord."

His attitude to pagan idolatry (v. 4). "Their sorrows shall be multiplied that hasten after another god: their drink-offerings of blood will I not offer, nor take up their names into My lips." When Rome occupied the land, they brought their pagan idolatry with them. Shrines were built at Tiberius and Caesarea Philippi. Our Lord's attitude was complete separation from it. It was at Caesarea Philippi, under the shadow of a heathen temple dedicated to the god Pan, that He tested His disciples as to His Person. It was after Peter's great confession: "Thou art the Christ, the Son of the living God," that He gave His great revelation of the Church, and added: "The gates of hell shall not prevail against it." One day idolatry is doomed to perish and fall before the triumphant banners of the Church, and the victory of the Son of Man, the Son of the living God.

His attitude to material things (vv. 5-6). He mentions five things: His portion, His lot, His cup, the lines, His goodly heritage. There is a possible reference to the inheritance of the Levite recorded in Numbers 18:20.

"I am *thy portion* and thine inheritance" (RV). Unlike the other tribes of Israel, who had a tract of land assigned to them, Levi had no such inheritance, but the Lord was their portion. Our Lord was the true Levite. The portion would be the over-all inheritance, what pertains to me in life.

The cup has to do with what I actually appropriate. David speaks of his overflowing cup (Ps. 23:5). We cannot forget the cup the Saviour had to drink, nor His promise to drink a new cup with His own in the coming kingdom.

The lot. When Israel was in the land, the plot assigned to the family was to be maintained and never sold or transferred. The priest and the Levite had no lot but the Lord Himself, however (Deut. 18:1-2).

The lines indicate a surveyor's line or linear measure, used for marking out property (Josh. 17:5; Micah 2:4-5). His lines were cast in pleasant places: Bethlehem, Bethany, Galilee, Hermon, Zion, Olivet. In these days of swift world-wide travel, it is well to remind ourselves that, apart from the journey into Egypt when He was a babe, our Lord's earthly ministry never took Him more than 120 miles from where He was born.

His attitude to the will of God (vv. 7-8). "I will bless the Lord, who hath given Me counsel: My reins also instruct Me in the night seasons. I have set the Lord always before Me: because

He is at My right hand, I shall not be moved." The Servant of Jehovah could declare in the words of Isaiah 50:4, "He wakeneth morning by morning, He wakeneth Mine ear to hear as the learned." Here we have a piece of soul-history. Whole nights were spent in prayer in communion with His Father. He could say, "My meat is to do the will of Him that sent Me, and to finish His work." And again, in His agony in Gethsemane, He cried: "Not My will, but Thine, be done." The whole section ends with the same idea as at the beginning. "I have set the Lord always before Me: because He is at My right hand, I shall not be moved." The Lord, and the fulfillment of His will was the object, the target of His life.

2. THE PATHWAY OF LIFE: HIS BURIAL, RESURRECTION, & EXALTATION (VV. 8-11)

This is the great Messianic section, quoted by the Apostles Peter and Paul in the New Testament and applied to the resurrection of Christ. At the incarnation, He is called "that Holy Thing" (Lk. 1:35) by the angel Gabriel; here He is called "Thine Holy One." Note four personal pronouns: My heart, My glory, My flesh, My soul. He is glad and rejoices, "For Thou wilt not leave My soul in Sheol, neither wilt Thou suffer Thine Holy One to see corruption." One speaks of His body and the other of His soul in the period between His death on the cross and His resurrection from the tomb.

There are two divergent views as to the meaning of the words: "Thou wilt not leave My soul in hell" (*sheol*). The Scofield Bible and very many orthodox and learned expositors of the Word take the passage in its plain, literal meaning, that our Lord, between His death and resurrection, descended into Sheol, described by our Lord in Luke 16:22 as Abraham's bosom, where Old Testament saints who died in faith were held until redemption's price, the precious blood of Christ, was paid.

There is no foundation for the notion that He offered or announced a second chance to those who died in rebellion against God (a misreading of 1 Peter 3:18-20).

The reasons for this view are as follows:

The description of Sheol-Hades in Luke 16:19-31 as a place of two compartments, Abraham's bosom for the saints, and the place of torment for the lost. It is a serious error to spiritualize or rationalize away our Lord's words.

The Old Testament saints at death went down: Jacob (Gen. 37:35; Job 14:13-15). Korah and company went down alive into the pit (Sheol). Samuel came up (1 Sam. 28:15). It was not his body which came up, for that was buried at Ramah, fifty miles away. It is true that Enoch and Elijah were raptured up into heaven, but they are clearly exceptional cases.

Peter says that David is not ascended into the heavens (Acts 2:34). Our Lord in resurrection said to Mary Magdalene: "I am not yet ascended to My Father" (Jn. 20:17). "Now that He ascended, what is it but that He...descended first into the lower parts of the earth?" (Eph. 4:9) This is the antithesis to "He that descended is the same also that ascended up far above all heavens, that He might fill all things" (v. 10). Remember that, in resurrection, the glorified Christ has at His girdle the keys of hell and of death (Rev. 1:18).

The intermediate state is not the grave. The grave is *qeber* or *shachath,* hell is Sheol or Hades. It means the unseen world of the departed spirits. The ancient Apostles' Creed says, "He descended into hell." This, of course, is not authoritative, but it shows that this view was held by the Church from ancient times.

The second view, held by many distinguished and honored teachers of the Word, is that when our Lord said: "Father, into Thy hands I commend My spirit," and bowed His head in death, He went to be with the Father in heaven, where He was between His death and resurrection. The Old Testament saints at death also went immediately to heaven.

David's comforting words are: "I will dwell in the house of the Lord forever." The fact that Moses and Elijah were taken up and that Moses appeared with the Lord in glory on the Mount of Transfiguration corroborates this.

It seems to the present writer that the weight of evidence appears to rest with the former view, that our Lord did descend to Sheol, where the Old Testament saints were confined, and at His resurrection and ascension He removed them to paradise above where they are today. But in questions of this kind, by all means let us have mutual love and affection and tolerance for those who hold either viewpoint.

There are some interesting and beautiful details in the New Testament concerning the burial of Christ. It is a part of the gospel, "and...He was buried" (1 Cor. 15:4).

We find the type in Leviticus 6:10-11, "And the priest shall put on his linen garment, and his linen breeches shall he put upon his flesh, and take up the ashes which the fire hath consumed with the burnt offering on the altar, and he shall put them beside the altar. And he shall put off his garments, and put on other garments, and carry forth the ashes without the camp unto a clean place."

Then we have the prophecy in Isaiah 53: "And He made His grave with the wicked, and with the rich in His death." They probably dug a grave at the foot of the cross in which He was to be unceremoniously buried. But God had other plans. The Gospels inform us that a rich man, Joseph of Arimathea, provided a rock-hewn tomb, and another secret disciple, Nicodemus, provided one hundred pounds of myrrh and aloes for the embalming. (Gamaliel, the renowned scholar, was said to be buried with eighty pounds of spices.)

After His death, no unholy hand touched that body. Man intended that He be buried with the malefactors, but Joseph provided the place and Nicodemus provided the perfume. Instead of the burial of a criminal, He was given the burial of a king (Cf., 2 Chron. 16:14).

"THOU WILT SHOW ME THE PATH OF LIFE" (V. 11)

Both Peter and Paul apply this to the resurrection of Christ in Acts 2:25-28 and Acts 13:35. There are eight passages in the Old Testament that clearly teach the resurrection of the body (Gen. 22:5; Job 19:23-27; Ps. 16:11; Ps. 17:14-15; Dan. 12:2-3, 13; Isa. 26:19; Hos. 13:14).

The resurrection of Christ is mentioned about 104 times in the New Testament. No other fact of Scripture is verified with such meticulous care. It is the best authenticated and attested event in the history of salvation. It is not an afterthought, an epilogue, or a codicil to the divine will and testament. First and last, it is the dominating testimony of the apostles.

The bodily resurrection of Jesus Christ has been called "the keystone of the arch of Christianity." Dislodge the keystone and all collapses. A brilliant agnostic in England said: "There is no use wasting time in discussing miracles. If bodily resurrection stands, all stands; if this goes, all goes."

The crucifixion loses its meaning without this. Without resurrection, His death is only that of a noble martyr. The resurrection of Christ is attributed to all three Members of the Holy Trinity: The Father (Rom. 6:4; Col. 2:12); The Son (Jn. 10:18; Lk. 24:6-7); The Holy Spirit (1 Pet. 3:18; Rom. 8:11).

FOUR ACCOUNTS OF THE RESURRECTION IN THE GOSPELS

All four Gospels record the resurrection of Christ. More space is given to it than to any other event, except the trial and the crucifixion. All four conclude with an account of His post-resurrection appearances. The charge of contradictions and discrepancies in the records is both ridiculous and superficial. The accounts dovetail and synchronize. They are not contradictory but complimentary. The ten appearances took place in five different spheres.

In a garden, the risen Lord appeared to a weeping woman,

Mary Magdalene. As Comforter, He wiped away her tears (Jn. 20:11-18). On a highway to two discouraged and disillusioned disciples, He came as the Companion on life's highway, He opened the Scriptures and revealed Himself to them (Lk. 24:13-31). In the upper room, He appeared in the midst of His fear-stricken disciples and showed Himself as the Gathering Center of His people (Jn. 20:19-23). By the seaside, He appeared to Simon Peter, the man who had so recently denied Him, and as the Confessor He restored and recommissioned him (Jn. 21:15-17). On the mountaintop in Galilee, as the Commissioner, He commanded His disciples to take the gospel to the whole world, and promised, "Lo, I am with you always, even to the end of the age" (Mt. 28:18-20).

THE RESURRECTION OF CHRIST IS THE THEME OF APOSTOLIC PREACHING

The resurrection is mentioned 21 times in the Acts. In all the apostolic sermons and addresses, it is not a mere appendage or accessory to the message, but the germ and kernel of the gospel. The apostles' primary function was to witness to the fact, and it was for this reason that they were persecuted and imprisoned. The Sadducees, who denied the possibility of resurrection, were the prime movers in this antagonism. Later, Paul suffered the same treatment from the philosophers at Athens (Acts 17:32) and the Roman governors. He is the author of the great exposition of the bodily resurrection of Christ in 1 Corinthians 15.

In Thy presence is fullness of joy (v. 11). It was for the joy set before Him that He endured the cross, despising the shame (Heb. 12:2). After His death, burial, and resurrection came His visible ascension to God's right hand. Joy mingled with heaviness and sorrow down here, but there was only full joy up there. This fullness of joy can now be experienced by His people when we abide in Him (Jn. 15:11). It comes also from fellowship with the Father and the Son, and with one another (1 Jn. 1:3-4).

And at His right hand there are pleasures for evermore. Here the position of our Lord in verse 8 is reversed. There Jehovah is at His right hand in communion and counsel during the time of His pathway of faith here below; now in the glory He is at the Father's right hand, the place of power, priesthood, and pleasure. There He awaits the coming home of His Bride.

8
Psalm 68
Psalm of the Ascension

PSALM 68

To the chief Musician.
A Psalm of David.

1 Let God arise, let His enemies be scattered: let them also that hate
Him flee before Him.
2 As smoke is driven away, so drive them away: as wax melteth be-
fore the fire, so let the wicked perish at the presence of God.
3 But let the righteous be glad; let them rejoice before God: yea, let
them exceedingly rejoice.
4 Sing unto God, sing praises to His name: extol Him that rideth
upon the heavens by His name JAH, and rejoice before Him.
5 A father of the fatherless, and a judge of the widows, is God in His
holy habitation.
6 God setteth the solitary in families: He bringeth out those which
are bound with chains: but the rebellious dwell in a dry land.
7 O God, when Thou wentest forth before Thy people, when Thou
didst march through the wilderness; Selah:

8 The earth shook, the heavens also dropped at the presence of God: even Sinai itself was moved at the presence of God, the God of Israel.
9 Thou, O God, didst send a plentiful rain, whereby Thou didst confirm Thine inheritance, when it was weary.
10 Thy congregation hath dwelt therein: Thou, O God, hast prepared of Thy goodness for the poor.
11 The Lord gave the word: great was the company of those that published it.
12 Kings of armies did flee apace: and she that tarried at home divided the spoil.
13 Though ye have lien among the pots, yet shall ye be as the wings of a dove covered with silver, and her feathers with yellow gold.
14 When the Almighty scattered kings in it, it was white as snow in Salmon.
15 The hill of God is as the hill of Bashan; an high hill as the hill of Bashan.
16 Why leap ye, ye high hills? this is the hill which God desireth to dwell in; yea, the LORD will dwell in it for ever.
17 The chariots of God are twenty thousand, even thousands of angels: the Lord is among them, as in Sinai, in the holy place.
18 Thou hast ascended on high, Thou hast led captivity captive: Thou hast received gifts for men; yea, for the rebellious also, that the LORD God might dwell among them.
19 Blessed be the Lord, who daily loadeth us with benefits, even the God of our salvation. Selah.
20 He that is our God is the God of salvation; and unto GOD the Lord belong the issues from death.
21 But God shall wound the head of His enemies, and the hairy scalp of such an one as goeth on still in his trespasses.
22 The Lord said, I will bring again from Bashan, I will bring My people again from the depths of the sea:
23 That thy foot may be dipped in the blood of thine enemies, and the tongue of thy dogs in the same.
24 They have seen Thy goings, O God; even the goings of my God,

my King, in the sanctuary.
25 The singers went before, the players on instruments followed after; among them were the damsels playing with timbrels.
26 Bless ye God in the congregations, even the Lord, from the fountain of Israel.
27 There is little Benjamin with their ruler, the princes of Judah and their council, the princes of Zebulun, and the princes of Naphtali.
28 Thy God hath commanded thy strength: strengthen, O God, that which Thou hast wrought for us.
29 Because of Thy temple at Jerusalem shall kings bring presents unto Thee.
30 Rebuke the company of spearmen, the multitude of the bulls, with the calves of the people, till every one submit himself with pieces of silver: scatter Thou the people that delight in war.
31 Princes shall come out of Egypt; Ethiopia shall soon stretch out her hands unto God.
32 Sing unto God, ye kingdoms of the earth; O sing praises unto the Lord; Selah:
33 To Him that rideth upon the heavens of heavens, which were of old; lo, He doth send out His voice, and that a mighty voice.
34 Ascribe ye strength unto God: His excellency is over Israel, and His strength is in the clouds.
35 O God, Thou art terrible out of Thy holy places: the God of Israel is He that giveth strength and power unto His people. Blessed be God.

PSALM OF THE ASCENSION

Psalms 42-72 comprise the second or Exodus section of the book of Psalms. Its subject is redemption. It contains three great Messianic psalms. Psalm 45 introduces us to the King-Bridegroom; Psalm 68 to the Ascended Man; and Psalm 69 to view the Trespass Offering. The book gives an outline of redemption in three main parts: deliverance from Egypt; the covenant at Sinai; and the sanctuary in the wilderness. All three are gathered up and summarized in Psalm 68. But it goes further, looking on to the establishment of the kingdom. It is a synopsis of history and prophecy. All the wealth of the divine names are poured into it. At the same time, it is full of difficulties, both for the interpreter and the expositor. The RV is a help in some of the more difficult sections.

Historically, J. G. Bellett places this psalm in 1 Chronicles 15, when David moved the ark from the house of Obed-Edom to Mount Zion. This is the song they sang. He says it is in six stages leading up to the mount. Psalms 24 and 132 are associated with the same period.

The psalm has its historical roots in the Old Testament and the doctrinal fruits in the New Testament. The Messianic reference (v. 18) is in dead center. The background seems to be four great victory marches, three historical and one prophetic.

AN OUTLINE OF PSALM 68

1. Introduction (vv. 1-6).
2. March out of Egypt to Sinai. The victory over the Egyptians is celebrated (vv. 7-8).
3. Victory over the Canaanites by Deborah and Barak is sung (vv. 9-19).
4. Bringing up the ark to Mount Zion (vv. 20-28).
5. Final victory and the establishment of the kingdom (vv. 29-35).

1. INTRODUCTION (VV. 1-6)

The psalm opens with almost an exact quotation of the words of Moses when the people of Israel set out on their wilderness journey: "Let God arise, let His enemies be scattered" (Num. 10:35). It was also the slogan of Cromwell's Roundheads as they went into battle. The name for God (Elohim) occurs six times in the introduction and twenty-six times in the psalm; also the majestic title "Jah" is used (v. 4). Two results of war are the widow and orphan, but the God of Israel takes care of them.

2. THE MARCH FROM EGYPT TO SINAI (VV. 7-8)

The presence of God is mentioned twice, both in the march through the wilderness and on Mount Sinai. After the redemption from Egypt and the victory over Pharaoh and his hosts, God brings His people to Sinai, where His glory is revealed and a covenant is entered into. This is the birthday of the nation and one of the most important events in Israel's history. As well as the law, the pattern of the Tabernacle is given, the place where God may dwell.

3. VICTORY OVER THE CANAANITE (VV. 9-19; JUD. 4-5)

There are many difficult words and expressions in the passage, pointed out by the experts, and dogmatism is out of place, but there seems to be a number of direct references to the victory over Sisera, the Canaanite described in Judges 4-5, and to some of the expressions in Deborah's song (ch. 5).

The storm: When Sisera invaded the land with nine hundred chariots of iron, the people were totally unprepared to stand up to an armored column. In the days of Shamgar and Jael, there was neither shield nor spear among the thousands of Israel (Jud. 5:6-8). But God intervened and the rain came down. The river Kishon overflowed its banks and the heavy iron chariots stuck in the mud and had to be abandoned. The Canaanite army fled on foot and were defeated by Barak and his men (Jud. 5:15, 21). It is still true that God is not always on the side of the big battalions! Napoleon learned that lesson when he invaded Russia: the winter snows came down and the flower of France was scattered and destroyed on the frozen steppes in the retreat from Moscow. Hitler refused to learn the lesson of history and suffered the same fate. A modern example is the Six-Day War in Israel in 1967.

The women dispatch riders (v. 11, RV). The men did the fighting, the women were in charge of communications.

The retreat, the rout, and the spoils of war (v. 12). Notice the change from the tedious labor among the sheepfolds to the golden raiment as a result of the victory!

The chariots of God are twenty thousand (v. 17). Sisera had nine hundred chariots of iron, but God's invincible, invisible army was there, as well as thousands of angels! Jael puts a tent peg through Sisera's head and the victory is complete. Barak leads his captivity captive (Jud. 5:12). Here the tables are turned: the Canaanites that had oppressed and enslaved the land for twenty years are now the prisoners of war.

4. DAVID'S VICTORY OVER THE JEBUSITES & PHILISTINES (VV. 20-28)

As soon as David had conquered the Jebusites, taken the city of Jerusalem, and made his home on Mount Zion, it was his consuming desire to provide a place for the ark of God. It had been captured by the Philistines in the time of the high priest Eli (1 Sam. 4:11). Owing to God's judgment on the Philistines, they returned it to Kirjath-jearim, where it remained for many years. David heard about it when he was a boy at Ephratah (Bethlehem) and determined that when he was in a position to do it, he would provide a temple for it in the center of the land (Ps. 132:1-9). Now this ambition was being fulfilled, and this section of Psalm 68 describes the song and the climax, as the procession and the ark, borne by the priestly Kohathites, ascend the hill and deposit the ark in the tent which David had pitched for it on Mount Zion (2 Sam. 6; 1 Chron. 15-16).

One of the great achievements of David during his reign was to unite all twelve tribes of the nation of Israel. Here the two southern tribes, Benjamin and Judah, are linked together with the two northern tribes, Zebulon and Naphtali, in a common purpose—to enthrone God in the sanctuary as the gathering center of His people in the land. Alas, it was not to last long. In the time of Jeroboam, the division took place, which will only be healed when the Son of David, the Prince of Peace, returns (Ezek. 37:15-28).

5. THE FINAL VICTORY, USHERING IN THE KINGDOM (VV. 29-35)

The three great historical victories in the psalm point forward to a coming mighty victory at Armageddon and the establishment of the kingdom with its earthly center at Jerusalem. "Because of Thy temple at Jerusalem shall kings bring presents unto Thee" (v. 29). "Scatter...the people that delight in war." War will be outlawed. "They shall beat their swords into plowshares, and their spears into pruning hooks: nation shall not lift up sword against nation, neither shall they learn war any more" (Isa. 2:4). "Princes shall come out of Egypt; Ethiopia shall soon stretch out her hands unto God." Countries that today conspire against and seek to destroy Israel will, in that day, have learned their lesson, and will bring tribute to the Sovereign and Just Ruler in Jerusalem. May the Lord hasten that day!

The Messianic passage (v. 18; Eph. 4:8) has five clauses: Thou hast ascended on high...Thou hast led captivity captive... Thou hast received gifts for men...For the rebellious also... That the Lord God might dwell among them.

"The 'rebellious' might be applied to Israel. The gospel was to the Jew first. Thank God, even today, there is a remnant of faith among them. But it can also be applied to ourselves, the Gentiles. "The rebellious"—that is what we were by nature; we were rebels against God. But the gift of salvation, and all other gifts, are for the rebellious. God laid all their rebellion and all their sins on His blessed Lamb, and having not withheld His only begotten Son, with Him He has given us all things" (Pettingill) .

"That the Lord God might dwell among them." This has always been God's great purpose, in the Tabernacle, in the Temple, in the Church, and in a coming day (Rev. 21:3).

In Paul's exposition of this great Messianic passage, he selects three clauses: Thou hast ascended on high; He led captivity captive; and gave gifts unto men.

Thou hast ascended on high—the ascension (Eph. 4:8). The main theme of the Epistle to the Ephesians is the Church as the body of Christ. He mentions it nine times. In chapter 4, the apostle concentrates on the unity of the body. It is in this context that we have the Messianic quotation from Psalm 68. In verse 3, we have the "unity of the Spirit," and in verse 13, "the unity of the faith." Ephesians 4 gives us God's method for bringing the organic unity of the Spirit and the doctrinal unity of the faith together. It comes from the ascended, glorified Head of the Church, our Lord Jesus Christ. The giving of gifts to the Church and their function in the body is the method that God uses.

There are sixteen passages in the New Testament that speak of the ascension of Christ. Three of these are historical and thirteen are doctrinal. Luke gives us three unique facts about it: *The locality*. It took place at Bethany on the Mount of Olives (Lk. 24:50). *The cloud* that received Him out of their sight (Acts 1:9), was it the Shekinah cloud that dipped down at His transfiguration and here again at His ascension? *The two men* who promised His coming back again, as they had seen Him go are also mentioned.

The word "up" is used seven times of His resurrection and His ascension: raised up (Acts 13:34); lifted up (Jn. 12:32); received up (Mk. 16:19); carried up (Lk. 24:51); taken up (Acts 1:9); went up (Acts 1:10); and ascended up (Eph. 4:10).

Ephesians 1:19-22 speaks of His resurrection and exaltation to the place of power at God's right hand. His ascension is linked with His priesthood, with His pouring out of the Holy Spirit, and with His Headship of the Church.

He led captivity captive (v. 8). Like a victorious general, He delivers those held captive by the enemy, then leads them in His triumphal victory march. He also distributes the booty, the spoils of war, to His troops. (See Gen. 14:16; Isa. 53:12; 2 Cor. 2:14; Heb. 2:15; 12:23.)

There are at least three interpretations of the passage:

a) In His death He defeated Satan and the satanic hosts, and liberated those that were held under this power. This He does in the gospel.

b) Old Testament saints, who up until His death and resurrection were in Sheol, in Abraham's bosom (Lk. 16:22), at His ascension were transferred to Paradise above.

c) Dwight Pentecost suggests a third interpretation. Leading captivity captive applies not to persons but to a principle. Christ triumphed over sin and death, and leads into freedom those who before were in bondage to sin and death.

Admittedly the passage is a difficult one and calls for consideration among those who may differ in their viewpoint. The present writer inclines towards the view expressed in number two, while gladly admitting the glorious truth of numbers one and three.

And gave gifts unto men (v. 8). There are three great gift passages in the New Testament:

a) Romans 12:4-8. Here the source of all gifts is God (v. 3).

b) 1 Corinthians 12. Here the operation of the Holy Spirit is emphasized (v. 7).

c) Ephesians 4:11. Here the gifts are bestowed by the ascended Christ (v. 8).

In Romans and 1 Corinthians, the gifts are endowments conferred on spiritual men; but in Ephesians the gifts are the men themselves given by the risen Head to the Church.

In Ephesians, the gifts are: apostle, prophet, evangelist, pastor, and teacher. In the primary sense, the apostle and prophet were in the foundation of the Church. An apostle in that sense was one who accompanied the Lord in His earthly ministry and was a witness of His resurrection (Acts 1:21-22). A prophet was one who was inspired by God and was responsible for conveying God's revelation to His people before the canon of Holy Scripture was completed.

In that primary sense we do not have the apostle and prophet with us today. In a secondary sense, we have men who are sent by God and those who minister to edification, exhortation, and comfort (1 Cor. 14:3). Also in the New Testament we have the apostles' doctrine and the completed revelation of God in His Word, and in that way the apostle and the prophet minister to us today.

We thank God that the other three gifts are with us today: the evangelist, the pastor, and the teacher. The men and their work have been set out in the following manner:

Evangelist	*Pastor*	*Teacher*
Philip	Timothy	Paul
Mobility	Stability	Ability
World	Local Church	Body of Christ
Merari	Gershom	Kohath

The fact that the last two, the pastor and the teacher, are linked together with the conjunction "and," might indicate that the two gifts could be combined in the same individual. However, the crying imperative need of the Church of God today is for these three gifted men and their work. We live in a day of dismal superficiality. It has been said that all true ministry has three ingredients: a supernatural gift from God; years of hard work and study in preparation; and experience in the school of suffering.

Finally, the ascended Christ confers gifts on the Church with an ultimate object in view. The Revised Version of verse 12 reads: "For the perfecting of the saints, unto the work of ministering, unto the building up of the body of Christ." The reason the gifts are given is that others may be trained in that work, and in the process the Church becomes self-propagating. According to God's plan, every local church should be a Bible training school, so that each generation passes on the torch to the next. This is the true apostolic succession.

9
Psalm 45
The King-Bridegroom

Psalm 45

To the chief Musician upon Shoshannim
for the sons of Korah, Maschil
A Song of loves

1 My heart is inditing a good matter: I speak of the things which I
have made touching the king: my tongue is the pen of a ready writ-
er.
2 Thou art fairer than the children of men: grace is poured into Thy
lips: therefore God hath blessed Thee for ever.
3 Gird Thy sword upon Thy thigh, O most mighty, with Thy glory
and Thy majesty.
4 And in Thy majesty ride prosperously because of truth and meek-
ness and righteousness; and Thy right hand shall teach Thee terrible
things.
5 Thine arrows are sharp in the heart of the king's enemies; whereby
the people fall under Thee.
6 Thy throne, O God, is for ever and ever: the sceptre of Thy king-

dom is a right sceptre.
7 Thou lovest righteousness, and hatest wickedness: therefore God, Thy God, hath anointed Thee with the oil of gladness above Thy fellows.
8 All Thy garments smell of myrrh, and aloes, and cassia, out of the ivory palaces, whereby they have made Thee glad.
9 Kings' daughters were among Thy honorable women: upon Thy right hand did stand the queen in gold of Ophir.
10 Hearken, O daughter, and consider, and incline thine ear; forget also thine own people, and thy father's house;
11 So shall the king greatly desire thy beauty: for He is thy Lord; and worship thou Him.
12 And the daughter of Tyre shall be there with a gift; even the rich among the people shall intreat thy favor.
13 The king's daughter is all glorious within: her clothing is of wrought gold.
14 She shall be brought unto the king in raiment of needlework: the virgins her companions that follow her shall be brought unto Thee.
15 With gladness and rejoicing shall they be brought: they shall enter into the king's palace.
16 Instead of thy fathers shall be thy children, whom thou mayest make princes in all the earth.
17 I will make Thy name to be remembered in all generations: therefore shall the people praise Thee for ever and ever.

THE KING-BRIDEGROOM

Psalm 45 is the seventh in the series, the center and crown of the Messianic psalms. There are six in the first book, presenting a basic Christology; the incarnation, temptation, betrayal, crucifixion, resurrection, and millennial glory of the Messiah. Psalm 45 introduces us to the marriage of the King and the glories that shall follow.

The title deserves our attention, coming in five phrases:

To the Chief Musician: This was the director of the temple music. Scripture mentions three of them: Asaph, Heman, and Ethan. This title is attached to fifty-five psalms. Ultimately Christ will be the chief musician of His people (Zeph. 3:17).

Upon Shoshannim: Meaning "lilies." Four psalms have this title. They are for the springtime and passover season. The winter is past, bringing in the world's spring and summer.

L'benai-Korah: By or for the Levitical family choir. They were the witnesses of divine judgment, the objects of divine grace (Num. 16; 1 Chron. 6:31-33). Eleven psalms in two series have this title.

Maschil: For teaching, or instruction. This title links the psalm with the last days (see Dan. 12:10). The wise *(maskilim)* shall understand.

A Song of loves: The Hebrew is in the plural. Kay gives "loveliness" or "beloved ones" *(yedidoth).* It is the word rendered "amiable" in Psalm 84:1. It is used especially of those loved by God (Deut. 33:12). It has been interpreted by Moffat as "a love song," by Young as a "song of beloved ones," in the Septuagint and the Vulgate as "a song of the beloved."

THE THEME AND TEACHING

Psalm 45 has been applied to some contemporary event, such as the marriage of Solomon to the daughter of Pharaoh, but as Perowne has remarked: "A greater than Solomon is here." Spurgeon's comment is: "Some see in this psalm only Solomon; they are shortsighted. Some see Solomon and Christ; they are cross-eyed. Well-focused spiritual eyes see Jesus only."

Hebrews 1:8-9 settles the Messianic interpretation. The quotation of verses 6 and 7 of the psalm, and its application to Christ in the Hebrews passage, makes any other interpretation inconsequential. Here we have the King and His bride coming forth after His marriage to deal with His enemies and to reign over the nations. "And He shall reign for ever."

In Psalm 91, we have the Prophet; in Psalm 110, it is the Priest; but in Psalm 45, it is the King. World events show that the imagery in the psalm will soon be realized. It is practical and not just devotional teaching. The rapture, the *bema,* the marriage supper, the apocalypse, and the reign of the King are all in the prophetic program and may soon be inaugurated by the shout of the Bridegroom.

The psalm gives a prophetic picture of Christ coming out to reign after the marriage supper (Rev. 19). He does not find the world waiting for Him. The world is in rebellion (Ps. 2). He brings a sword and a scepter with Him.

AN OUTLINE OF PSALM 45

There are two principal parts with a brief introduction and conclusion:

1. Introduction (v. 1).
2. Fourfold glory of the King-Bridegroom (vv. 2-8)
3. Fourfold beauty of the Bride-consort (vv. 9-15).
4. Conclusion (vv. 16-17) with a twofold blessing of the Bridegroom mentioned.

1. INTRODUCTION (V. 1)

One verse suffices for the preface, but the speaker uses four figures of his feelings about his theme: His heart is a bubbling fountain. His mouth is that of the orator. His theme is the musical composition of a poet. His tongue is the facile pen of the scribe. He uses every faculty to extol the glories of the King.

2. THE FOURFOLD GLORY OF THE KING-BRIDEGROOM (VV. 2-8)

His Moral Glory. Two items are included: He is fairer than the children of men; and grace is poured into His lips. Here we have an overview of His Person and His ministry—what He is, and what He said. "Fairer" is a coined word. It is said to have no parallel in Hebrew construction. Some render the word, "beautiful, beautiful!" or "fairer far." He is contrasted with other sons of men. He is the prototype; the perfect, typical, representative Man; the Son of Man. Enoch, Joseph, David, all come short. He is the perfect pattern, physically and morally.

Every nation and age has its hero. Moses, Nebuchadnezzar, Alexander, Augustus Caesar, Socrates, Napoleon, Bismarck, Shakespeare, Washington. They represent the genius of a nation incarnate in a man—Israel, Babylon, Greece, Rome, France, Germany, England, America. But He is not in that class. He is a Man outside of time, above time, the God-Man. He is fair in aspect and gracious in speech. Good to look at, and good to listen to!

"Grace is poured into Thy lips." First we see the vessel, then what is poured in. Only one item of His life and ministry is selected: "And all bare Him witness, and wondered at the gracious words which proceeded out of His mouth" (Lk. 4:22). His moral glory was in perfect balance: wisdom and simplicity, gentleness and indignation, grace and truth. We are all creatures of extremes, but His moral perfection was in perfect equilibrium, like the two wings of a bird. Moses was the meekest man in all the earth, but he spoke unadvisedly with his tongue. But in Christ every grace was manifest in perfection: courtesy, consideration, compassion, and kindness. Grace is said to be the most beautiful word in our language. It is used only twice in the Psalms. Here it is poured into His lips. In Psalm 84, it is a gift conferred on the pilgrim (v. 11).

His Official Glory. There are four items included: His sword, scepter, throne, and anointing. First, it is His moral glory as Man, then His official glory as King. Here the grace of His public ministry is exchanged for the girded sword. He gains the kingdom, not by the penetrating power of the gospel, but by conquest. At His apocalypse and epiphany the hostile forces of hell and antichrist, described in Psalm 2:1-3, are arrayed against Him. The conflict is graphically described in Zechariah 14 and Revelation 19.

His scepter, representing power and authority in government, is the shepherd's rod, which has become an iron rod for His enemies, but a golden scepter for His people. He is anointed with the oil of gladness above His fellows.

David was anointed three times as king; first in the house of his father, Jesse; secondly, when Saul was dead, over the royal tribe of Judah; and thirdly, over the twelve tribes of Israel at Hebron. Our Lord was anointed twice while He was here on earth, once at the beginning of His public ministry (Lk. 7:38), and again at the end (Jn. 12:3). The anointing with the oil of gladness could refer to His anointing with the Holy Spirit (Lk. 4:18). But who are the "fellows" of verse 7? It has been suggested that they are the other occupants of the throne of David. Some were good and some were bad, but all were human, while He is divine.

His Divine Glory (v. 6). "Thy throne, O God, is for ever and ever." This is one of the most outstanding passages concerning the deity of the King. No wonder it has been attacked! The ASR renders it: "Your divine throne endures forever and ever." But the writer of the Hebrews says: "Unto the Son He saith, Thy throne, O God, is for ever and ever." Both the Old Testament and the interpretation of the New Testament apply the passage to Christ. The modernist says, "the ancients deified their kings." Pagan Rome did, but Israel never. It is a dishonor to Christ to delete God from the text and apply divinity to the throne instead of to the Person. Interpretation is lifted out of the realm of speculation by Hebrews 1:8.

His Mediatorial Glory (vv. 8-9). Three items should be noted in this section:

Out of the ivory palaces (v. 8)—the Incarnation. An ivory palace is the last word in opulence. King Ahab had an ivory palace in Samaria (1 Ki. 22:39). Ivory comes from the death of earth's largest, noblest creature. The ivory palace speaks of the glory which our Lord left when He stooped to be born in Bethlehem.

In some hymnbooks which have the hymn by Henry Barraclough, "Out of the Ivory Palaces," under the title are printed these words: "Suggested by a sermon by Dr. J. Wilbur Chapman on Psalm 45:8, in which Christ is pictured coming out of the ivory palaces of Heaven to redeem mankind, clothed in garments which are perfumed with myrrh for beauty, aloes for bitterness, cassia for healing, the fragrance of which remains to tell of His near presence."

All Thy garments smell of myrrh...aloes, and cassia (v. 8). In verse 8 He comes out of the ivory palaces with a symphony of stringed instruments. But in verse 15 He goes into the King's palace with a song of gladness and rejoicing. How is this made possible? The garments explain.

At His birth, the wise men brought presents of gold, frankincense, and myrrh. There was fragrance at His birth, and fragrance in His life. At His burial, Nicodemus brought one hundred pounds of myrrh and aloes to place upon that holy body. There was fragrance at His death, burial, and resurrection. So here again His royal robes are fragrant with spices.

At His right hand—the Queen. This is the result of His work on the cross. The introduction of the queen is the point of transition between the two parts of the psalm.

Summary: In the description of the King-Bridegroom we have His moral glory as a Man, His official glory as a King, His divine glory as God, and His mediatorial glory as the Bridegroom. We see the excellency of His Person, the equity of His rule, the eternity of His throne, and the ecstacy of His heart. All remind us of the hymn: "Majestic sweetness sits enthroned upon the Saviour's brow" by Samuel Stennett.

3. THE FOURFOLD BEAUTY OF THE BRIDE (VV. 9-15)

Her name: The queen (v. 9). This is the Hebrew word, *shegal,* not the usual *malkah* or *gebireh.* "It is a rare and unusual designation of a consort of the first rank." *Shegal is* used of Chaldean or Persian queens (Dan. 5:2-3; Neh. 2:6). This would seem to indicate that the queen-consort here is a Gentile. (Cf., Joseph and Boaz and their Gentile brides.)

The usual interpretation is that the bride in the psalm is Israel, forgiven and restored in her relation to Messiah in millennial days. But the word used for "queen" in verse 9, and the prophetic outline in Revelation 19-22, concerning the marriage supper of the Lamb and the appearing in glory followed by the millennium, make that interpretation difficult, if not impossible. Israel, it is true, will have a special and intimate relationship with the Messiah as an earthly people, with an earthly center in Jerusalem, but the bride is the Church, composed of both Jew and Gentile, and in that relationship will reign over the earth in the New Jerusalem which comes from God out of heaven. Both Israel and the Church have a glorious future in relation to the King in that millennial day. When we keep these distinctions clearly in our minds, most of the difficulties vanish.

Her attendants: They are the Kings' daughters (v. 9), and the daughter of Tyre shall be there with a gift (v. 12). These are the matrons and maids of honor. Tyre was the queen city of commerce. Here she comes, not with a bill, but with a bridal gift. The rich are not now proud and domineering, but humbly entreating His face. Surely a changed world! The virgins, her companions (v. 14) might represent Gentile nations, evangelized and brought into millennial blessing through Israel.

Her attire: The King's daughter is all glorious within! It is what we are within that matters most. Her clothing is of:

Gold of Ophir (v. 9). This may speak of her standing. The

wedding garment is imputed righteousness. Our Great High Priest has garments of gold and linen woven together.

Jesus, Thy blood and righteousness,
My beauty are, my glorious dress.
Midst flaming worlds in these arrayed,
With joy shall I lift up my head. —*N. L. von Zinzedorf*

Wrought gold (v. 13). Here her beauty is the result of the hammer and the heat—the school of suffering that can produce such inner glory when we are exercised by the disciplines of God.

The garment of needlework (v. 14). This is the embroidery of a life of service. Stitch by stitch, the righteous acts of saints prepare the Church for her wedding day (Rev. 19:8).

Her attitude. Note the fourfold bridal charge (vv. 10-11):

a) "Forget...thine own people, and thy father's house." Adam and his posterity are no longer where our loyalty lies. The old life and habits are to be gone. (Cf., Ruth and Moab, Ruth 1:16-17).

b) "So shall the king greatly desire thy beauty." This is the sweetness of communion. Her beauty is to be for Him alone.

c) "For He is thy Lord." Complete subjection to His word and will is the path of joy and fulfillment.

d) "Worship thou Him." Her devotional life is centered on Him. "Set your affections on things above, where Christ sits."

She is to hearken, consider, incline, and forget. There has to be renunciation, choices to be made, irrevocable allegiance to be registered, never to turn back (Mt. 10:37).

THE BRIDAL PROCESSION (VV. 14-15)

"Stringed instruments have made thee glad." A burst of praise and jubilation welcomes the King's arrival. Then the queen-bride with her virgin companions are brought into the

King's palace (v. 15). This is followed by a charge to the King-Bridegroom (vv. 16-17). The three pronouns are all masculine: thy fathers, thy children, thy name.

Thy fathers. This speaks of the old Jewish economy, and of the patriarchs.

Thy children: The individuals who make up the Church are addressed as such (Heb. 2:13), for He shall see His seed (Isa. 53:10) in spite of the fact that He was cut off in death. The phrase, "whom Thou mayest make princes in all the earth" speaks of the places of administration in the kingdom. "We shall reign with Him."

Thy Name. No more will that Name be used in derision and shame. Finally eternal praise linked with it. Thus this great psalm ends with a benediction associated with the Name:

There is a Name I love to hear, I love to speak its worth;
It sounds like music in mine ear, the sweetest Name on earth.

And now the divine benediction at the conclusion of the ceremony. The royal nuptials are regarded as over and the Bridegroom is addressed by God. The benediction concerns the perpetuation of the royal race and the exaltation of the eternal King. "A seed shall serve Him; and they shall be counted unto the Lord for a generation." The promise of Isaiah 53:10 will then be fulfilled: "He shall see His seed, He shall prolong His days, and the pleasure of the Lord shall prosper in His hand." His spiritual posterity will outshine His human progenitors in honor, power, and glory. "His name will be remembered in all generations and His praise shall never cease."

10
Psalm 24
The King of Glory

PSALM 24

A Psalm of David

1 The earth is the LORD's, and the fulness thereof; the world, and
they that dwell therein.
2 For He hath founded it upon the seas, and established it upon the
floods.
3 Who shall ascend into the hill of the LORD? or who shall stand in
His holy place?
4 He that hath clean hands, and a pure heart; who hath not lifted up
his soul unto vanity, nor sworn deceitfully.
5 He shall receive the blessing from the LORD, and righteousness
from the God of his salvation.
6 This is the generation of them that seek Him, that seek Thy face, O
Jacob. Selah.
7 Lift up your heads, O ye gates; and be ye lift up, ye everlasting
doors; and the King of glory shall come in.
8 Who is this King of glory? The LORD strong and mighty, the

LORD mighty in battle.
9 Lift up your heads, O ye gates; even lift them up, ye everlasting doors; and the King of glory shall come in.
10 Who is this King of glory? The LORD of hosts, He is the King of glory. Selah.

THE KING OF GLORY

It has often been pointed out that Psalms 22, 23, and 24 form a trilogy covering the past, present, and future. They speak of Christ as the Sufferer, the Shepherd, and the Sovereign. They remind us of the altar in the tabernacle court, the table in the holy place, and the throne in the holiest of all.

Psalm 24 has been interpreted in a threefold way:

a) *Historically.* The story is being told of the bringing up of the ark of God to Zion (2 Sam. 6).

b) *Typically.* The ascension of the Lord Jesus back to the Father's right hand. Spurgeon calls it "the song of the ascension." George Handel, in his wonderful oratorio, *Messiah,* also applies it in this way.

c) *Prophetically.* It is seen as an outline of the Lord's coming in glory when He will establish His throne in the very city where He was rejected and condemned.

Psalm 24, however, is an earthly scene, not heavenly. The hill, the house, and the holy place are literal. The psalm presupposes an empty throne, the throne of world dominion, and a challenge as to who has the qualifications to occupy it.

There are a number of thrones in Scripture:

a) The throne of God. Mentioned many times in the Old and New Testaments, it speaks of His right, power, and ability to rule over all.

b) The throne of grace (Heb. 4:16). In the present age of

grace, the Lord sits in glory, available to help His people in every time of need.

c) The throne of glory (Mt. 25:31). This refers to the judgment of the nations in a coming day. The One who sits upon the throne will not only do right; He will be *seen* to do right.

d) The great white throne of judgment (Rev. 20:11) points to the final assize, when the dead, small and great will stand before the Judge to hear sentence passed.

e) The throne of God and the Lamb (Rev. 22:1) is the administrative center of heaven, when all will be set right.

But on the earthly level, there is another throne, that of world dominion. It has been occupied for many centuries by the Gentiles. Many tyrants and ambitious, bloodthirsty adventurers have presumed to sit on it, but in present-day confusion and chaos it is empty. Psalm 24 answers the question as to who has the right to occupy it.

The psalm calls Him "the King of glory." The title occurs five times in the psalm, and is found nowhere else in Scripture. The term, "the God of glory," is used in Acts 7:2; "the Lord of glory" in 1 Corinthians 2:8; and "the Father of glory" in Ephesians 1:17. But only here do we have "the King of glory."

AN OUTLINE OF PSALM 24

The psalm is in two parts, divided by the *selah* of verse 6.

1. The challenge and the credentials for world dominion (vv. 1-6).

2. The conqueror enters the city and the sanctuary (vv. 7-10).

1. CHALLENGE AND CREDENTIALS FOR WORLD DOMINION (VV. 1-6)

The Challenge: "Who shall ascend into the hill of the Lord?

or who shall stand in His holy place?" (v. 3)

There are two eminences in the city of Jerusalem, Mount Zion with the royal palace to the south, and Mount Moriah with the temple site to the north: these are the hill and the house of the psalm. The candidate to take possession of them must be both a king and a priest.

Jerusalem is destined to be the metropolis of the world during the millennium. Ezekiel gives a detailed description of a re-erected temple, with a revived worship, and a river flowing out of the sanctuary (Ezek. 40-48). At the same time, the Davidic covenant guaranteed a dynasty, a throne, and a kingdom in perpetuity (2 Sam. 7:8-17; Ps. 89:20-37). The challenge therefore is: who has the credentials and the qualifications to occupy the royal palace and at the same time to function as a priest in the temple?

The Moral Credentials of the Lord: (vv. 4-5) "He that hath clean hands, and a pure heart; who hath not lifted up his soul unto vanity, nor sworn deceitfully. He shall receive the blessing from the LORD, and righteousness from the God of his salvation." Here are four moral qualifications required of the person worthy to occupy the hill and the house.

The first applicant was Satan. At our Lord's temptation in the wilderness, he claimed to have possession of all the kingdoms of this world and the glory of them (Lk. 4:5-6). But clearly that was a usurper's claim and he certainly does not fulfill the credentials or qualifications.

Then we have the four great Gentile world empires of Babylon, Medo-Persia, Greece, and Rome, with the names of Nebuchadnezzar, Cyrus, Alexander, and Augustus Caesar. In more modern times there have been Napoleon, Hitler, Stalin, and Mao. When we compare them with the required moral qualifications, we see how far short they come.

Adolf Hitler boasted that he would found an empire that would last a thousand years. Does he have clean hands? They are stained with the blood of six million Jews cruelly done to death in the gas ovens of Europe. Does Nero, the Roman emperor have a pure heart? He was a human monster who murdered his own mother and who killed his wife with a kick when she was pregnant with his unborn child.

Napoleon lifted up his soul unto vanity. When he was being crowned emperor, it was suggested to him that the pope should be invited to perform the ceremony. This he disdainfully refused, and with inflated pride, set the crown on his own head.

Stalin swore deceitfully when he signed political alliances and later broke them. He, too, is said to have been responsible for the planned extermination of eleven million persons in the Ukraine and other parts of Russia.

Certainly none of these would-be rulers fulfill the moral qualifications to occupy the throne of world dominion. But let us think of another Man—Jesus of Nazareth. Does He meet the standard?

Did He have clean hands? His hands were pure, powerful, pierced, and priestly hands. They were laid in compassion on the leper, on the blind, and on the heads of little children while He blessed them.

Did He have a pure heart? He was sinless and impeccable. There was no traitor within the gates of His mind or heart to open the door to the tempter. He could throw out the challenge to the world: "Which of you convinceth Me of sin?" (Jn. 8:46) There was no answer to that challenge.

Was His soul lifted up unto vanity? He could say: "I am meek and lowly in heart" (Mt. 11:29). Pride was Satan's original sin. He reached up, but Jesus stooped down to the death of the cross.

Did He ever swear deceitfully? He was truth personified. He could say: "I am the way, the truth, and the life: no man cometh unto the Father, but by Me" (Jn. 14:6).

All the political leaders who have ever appeared in this world have failed the moral test: the only One who has come up to the standard is Jesus of Nazareth. He is the only perfect moral Person the world has ever seen.

Alexander Maclaren has written: "Of the four aspects of purity, the two central refer to the inward life, embedded in the outward life of deeds and words. The hands are neither red with blood, nor foul with grubbing in the dunghills for gold. The outward is only right when the inward disposition is pure."

His Creatorial Right to the Throne: "The earth is the Lord's, and the fulness thereof; the world, and they that dwell therein" (vv. 1-2). The first refers to the material and mineral wealth stored up in this planet: gold, silver, iron, copper, diamonds, etc. Then coal, oil, electricity, water, and atomic power. Then the resources in field and forest: vegetables, plants, and crops—everything to enrich the environment and to make human and animal life possible and enjoyable.

Secondly, He has a right to the world's population, "they that dwell therein." Today there are about one hundred twenty nations with billions of people. There are three thousand seventy-six named languages in the world and several thousand lesser dialects. And every tongue will some day confess Him as Lord (Phil. 2).

Paul uses five prepositions to describe the creatorial work of Christ (Col. 1:16-17). In Him *(en);* by Him *(dia);* for Him *(eis);* He is before *(pros)* all things; by Him *(en)* all things consist (or hold together). This tremendous statement shows that He is the Creator and Sustainer of the universe. Paul teaches that He is also the Redeemer and Reconciler.

His Redemptive Rights: As well as the character credentials and the creatorial rights to sit on the throne of world dominion, the Saviour has purchased that which was lost through the Fall. Our mighty Man of wealth, far greater than Boaz, has redeemed us to God by His blood.

Associated with Him is a generation that seeks God's face (v. 6). The Septuagint and Syriac versions have: "O God of

Jacob." (For the collective use of Jacob's name, see Num. 23:7ff; Deut. 32:9; Ps. 44:4; 47:4.) There seem to be two distinct thoughts: those seeking Jehovah are the true Israel, and when the nations see Israel going after Jehovah, they go after Israel, too. (For this second company see Zech. 8:23; Isa. 55:5.)

2. THE CONQUEROR ENTERS THE CITY & SANCTUARY (VV. 7-10)

The church age and the rapture do not come into Psalm 24. The prophetical background to the psalm is Revelation 4-19. The rapture of the Church, followed by the seven-year period, occupied with the beginning of sorrows (Mt. 24:8) and the great tribulation (Mt. 24:21), have already taken place. The climax is the appearing in glory of the Messiah, when He deals with His enemies at the battle of Armageddon, and reveals Himself to the nation of Israel, who up until that point have rejected His claims as the Messiah. But now repentant and restored, they join His victorious train.

The last two Messianic prophesies of the Old Testament are: "Behold, I will send My Messenger, and He shall prepare the way before Me: and the Lord, whom ye seek, shall suddenly come to His temple, even the messenger of the covenant, whom ye delight in" (Mal. 3:1). "But unto you that fear My name shall the Sun of Righteousness arise with healing in His wings" (Mal. 4:2). The second section of Psalm 24 gives the fulfillment of these great prophecies.

After the mighty victory at Armageddon, the deliverance of Israel, and their repentance and conversion, the Conqueror and His retinue approach the gates of the city of Jerusalem. They are bolted and barred against the enemy. The herald calls out: "Lift up your heads, O ye gates: and be ye lift up, ye everlasting doors; and the King of glory shall come in!" The reply from inside the walls is: "Who is this King of glory?" The answer from the herald is: "The Lord, strong and mighty, the Lord mighty in battle!"

There are three great battles which He won: over Satan at His temptation in the wilderness; over the hosts of hell on the cross; and over the enemies of God at Armageddon. Then the gates are thrown wide open and He comes in and occupies the city and the royal palace.

Again the cortege moves on to the temple site. It was here that He was rejected at His first coming, lowly and riding upon an ass. Now He rides the white horse and the messenger of the covenant suddenly comes to His temple.

Again the challenge from the herald: "Lift up your heads, O ye gates; and be ye lift up, ye everlasting doors; and the King of glory shall come in!" and the inquiry from within the sanctuary: "Who is this King of glory?" The majestic answer is: "The Lord of hosts [Jehovah-Sabaoth], He is the King of glory!" This is the term used in Isaiah 6:5 for the occupant of the throne in the Temple. Isaiah cried: "Mine eyes have seen the King, the Lord of hosts." Then the King enters and takes possession of the house. The hill and the house are occupied by the King of Glory.

When our Lord came in humiliation at His first advent, He was designated "King of the Jews." Such was His title in rejection. In His manifestation in the millennium, He will be King of kings and Lord of lords. But in relation to His people, He is the King of glory. He will be the Priest-King, "a Priest upon His throne, and He shall bear the glory" (Zech. 6:12-13).

11
Psalm 110
The Priest-King-Judge

Psalm 110

A Psalm of David

1 The LORD said unto My Lord, Sit Thou at My right hand, until I
make Thine enemies Thy footstool.
2 The LORD shall send the rod of Thy strength out of Zion: rule
Thou in the midst of Thine enemies.
3 Thy people shall be willing in the day of Thy power, in the beau-
ties of holiness from the womb of the morning: Thou hast the dew of
Thy youth.
4 The LORD hath sworn, and will not repent, Thou art a priest for
ever after the order of Melchizedek.
5 The Lord at Thy right hand shall strike through kings in the day of
His wrath.
6 He shall judge among the heathen, He shall fill the places with the
dead bodies; He shall wound the heads over many countries.
7 He shall drink of the brook in the way: therefore shall He lift up
the head.

THE PRIEST-KING-JUDGE

Psalm 110 is quoted in the New Testament fourteen times, more frequently than any other Old Testament passage, and in each case is applied to our Lord Jesus Christ. It is not only the Apostles Peter and Paul and the author of the Epistle to the Hebrews who make this identification, but we have the authority of our Lord Himself, who said it was written by David under the inspiration of the Holy Spirit (Mt. 22:41-46). His argument turned on two points: first, that David was the author of the psalm; and secondly, that David, inspired by the Spirit of God, called his son his Lord. The Pharisees got the point and made no attempt to dispute it.

The psalm follows Psalm 109, where the Messiah is presented as the "poor and needy" man. Here He is the exalted Lord.

"The 110th Psalm gives us the key to history. The One who alone can right the wrongs of earth, hush its storms, break its chains, heal its wounds, straighten out its crookedness, dispel its darkness, is hidden in heaven, because there was no room for Him on earth. Sitting at the right hand of God, the exclusive privilege of the Son and Heir, He is patiently biding His time, till the hour when God will intervene on His behalf on earth, making His enemies the footstool of His feet" (Max Isaac Reich).

AN OUTLINE OF PSALM 110

The psalm gives three magnificent pictures of Christ, ending with a delightful appendix:

1. As Priest exalted to God's right hand (v. 1), He waits expectantly.

2. As King-Priest, He is commanded to rule (vv. 2-4), and shall—resplendent in His glory.

3. As Judge, He deals with His enemies (vv. 5-6). He, the

Patient One, shall be triumphant at last.

4. The Appendix: The drink and the uplifted head (v. 7).

We find a magnificent statement of deity at the beginning, a delightful touch of humanity at the end.

Notice that the psalm commences with two striking commands: "Sit Thou!" (v. 1), for two thousand years on His Father's throne. "Rule Thou!" (v. 2), for one thousand years on the millennial throne.

1. AS PRIEST EXALTED TO GOD'S RIGHT HAND (V. 1)

"The Lord said unto My Lord, sit Thou at My right hand, until I make Thine enemies Thy footstool." "The oracle of Jehovah unto my Adonai." Gifford says that the opening words are robbed of their force in the Authorized. The term is used constantly by the prophets in the Old Testament to introduce a solemn oracle of Jehovah. It is used only here in the Psalms. Its first occurrence is in Genesis 22:16: "By Myself have I sworn, saith Jehovah." It is the highest claim to inspiration. Our English language is a poor medium to transmit the majesty of the utterance.

David, speaking by the Spirit, gives us a scene in the councils of the Godhead, between the Father and the Son. In response to the command, "Sit Thou at My right hand," four times in the Epistle to the Hebrews we see the Son sitting down at God's right hand.

a) *As the sin-purger,* greater than the prophets, the One in whom God has given the final and complete revelation (Heb. 1:1-5).

b) *As the High Priest* who enables us to draw nigh to God (Heb. 8:1-2).

c) *As the One who has completed His sacrificial work,* having by His one offering perfected forever them that are sanctified (Heb. 10:1-12).

d) *As the Pioneer and Perfecter of faith,* He is the example and inspiration of a like faith in His people (Heb. 12:1-3).

The priesthood of Christ in Hebrews is presented in a twofold way. First, it is after the pattern of Aaron; secondly, it is after the order of Melchizedek.

The sacrificial phase of Aaron's priesthood was performed at the brazen altar. At the ritual on the Day of Atonement, described in Leviticus 16, Aaron entered the holiest three times, dressed in a white linen garment: first, with the incense which he placed before the mercy seat (Heb. 9:4); secondly, with the blood of a bullock which he offered for himself and his family; finally, with the blood of the sin offering, which he sprinkled once on the mercy seat and seven times before it. This typified the great work of propitiation towards God.

Then he came out to the altar where the live scapegoat was standing. Placing his hands on its head, he confessed all the sins, iniquities, and transgressions of the people, and the goat was led away by a fit man into the wilderness, into a land not inhabited. This typified substitution and the removal of the sin confessed.

The sprinkled blood inside was propitiation towards God, the sin confessed and transferred and taken away was substitution. Both together are pictures of the sacrificial work of Christ on the cross.

Then Aaron went inside the holy place and changed his garments to those of glory and beauty. He placed the priestly miter, with the words, "HOLINESS TO THE LORD," inscribed on a golden plate, upon his head. Then the blue robe with the linen ephod was placed on top. On his shoulders he bore the names of the twelve tribes collectively engraven on two onyx stones, and the breastplate with the twelve names of the tribes individually on twelve precious, variegated colored stones, each enclosed in gold, upon his heart. Finally, the sash was wrapped around his waist. In these robes he represented the people as intercessor before God.

At the end of this great day, he came out, and after offering a final sacrifice upon the altar, he lifted up his hands and blessed the people with the priestly blessing: "The Lord bless thee, and keep thee: The Lord make His face [to] shine upon thee, and be gracious unto thee: The Lord lift up His countenance upon thee, and give thee peace" (Num. 6:24-26).

Hebrews 9 is the fulfillment of the Day of Atonement, commencing with the censer inside the veil, and ending with the words: "So Christ was once offered to bear the sins of many; and unto them that look for Him shall He appear the second time without sin unto salvation."

As Priest today on the throne, He has a threefold work for His people:

a) *As Advocate,* He takes care of our sins. "My little children, these things write I unto you, that ye sin not. And if any man sin, we have an Advocate with the Father, Jesus Christ the righteous" (1 Jn. 2:1).

b) *As our Intercessor,* He takes care of our supplications. "But this man, because He continueth ever, hath an unchangeable priesthood. Wherefore He is able also to save them to the uttermost that come unto God by Him, seeing He ever liveth to make intercession for them" (Heb. 7:24-25).

c) *As our Great High Priest,* He takes care of our sorrows. "Seeing then that we have a great high priest, that is passed into the heavens, Jesus the Son of God, let us hold fast our profession. For we have not an high priest which cannot be touched with the feeling of our infirmities; but was in all points tempted like as we are, yet without sin. Let us therefore come boldly unto the throne of grace, that we may obtain mercy, and find grace to help in time of need" (Heb. 4:14-16).

While the priesthood of Christ in His sacrifice and intercession is after the pattern of Aaron, yet it is also in contrast to it. In many things Aaron failed; he never sat down, his sacrifices had to be offered every year, and finally he had to lay aside his priestly robes and die. But our Great High Priest was sinless, He has sat down on the throne, and He has offered one sacrifice for sins forever.

So the first verse of the psalm covers the high priestly work of Christ at God's right hand today, but it continues until His enemies are put under His feet and made His footstool. That would extend to the rapture, the judgment seat of Christ, and His appearing in glory. It will end when God gives the second command: "Rule Thou in the midst of Thine enemies."

2. AS KING-PRIEST (VV. 2-4)

The command, "Sit Thou" (v. 1) is followed by "Rule Thou" (v. 2). This would refer to the millennial reign of Christ, which will last for a period of one thousand years (Rev. 20:1-6). "The Lord shall send the rod of Thy strength out of Zion." The "rod" is the shepherd's rod. It was Moses' symbol of authority when he was sent by God to confront Pharaoh. With it he opened the waters of the Red Sea and smote the rock, out of which the living waters flowed (Ex. 4:2-4; 7:19; 8:5, 16-17; 14:16). It is called a rod of iron in Psalm 2:9 and in Revelation 2:27. In a monarchy, on his coronation day, the scepter is placed in the sovereign's hand as a symbol of authority in government. In millennial days, Christ will be an absolute monarch with supreme powers and control.

"Thy people shall be freewill offerings in the day of Thy power" (v. 3). This would indicate a Jewish remnant which will welcome Him when He comes in glory to reign. At His first advent, "He came unto His own, [but] His own received Him not" (Jn. 1:11). After the rapture of the Church, God will open the eyes of a remnant of Israel, as to the true meaning of Isaiah 53 and the Messianic hope. Like Paul's dramatic conversion on the road to Damascus, they too will be illuminated by the Spirit of God. They will be sealed and preserved during tribulation days and will be God's testimony on earth during the time of Jacob's trouble. They will be the preachers of the gospel of the kingdom, and, in a very real sense, freewill offerings to God in their consecration and dedication to Him.

The latter part of verse 3, "in the beauties of holiness from the womb of the morning: Thou hast the dew of Thy youth," is not so easy to understand and interpret. The womb of the morning is a poetic phrase pointing to that morning without a cloud, when Christ shall come in glory, and the Sun of Righteousness shall arise with healing in His wings. It is the appearing, the apocalypse, and the epiphany, the outshining of His glory described in Revelation 19:11-16 and in Zechariah 14:3-4. The hosts of heaven shall issue forth with the glorified Christ at their head.

His retinue is first described. The phrase, "in the beauties of holiness," corresponds, in regard to character, to the arraying of priests in holy garments. The saints, who will be with Christ in the day of His manifested glory as the Priest-King, will themselves constitute a royal priesthood. Addressing His people Israel, the Lord said: "Ye shall be unto Me a kingdom of priests, and an holy nation" (Ex. 19:6). Concerning the Church, the Apostle Peter says: " But ye are a chosen generation, a royal priesthood, a holy nation (1 Pet. 2:9). The Apostle John in the opening doxology of Revelation, says: "Unto Him that loveth us, and loosed us from our sins by His blood; and He made us to be a kingdom, to be priests unto His God and Father; to Him be the glory and the dominion for ever and ever. Amen" (Rev. 1:5-6, RV).

Some would apply the last phrase of verse 3, "Thou hast the dew of thy youth," to this company of priestly attendants, and use the marginal reading: "thy youth are to Thee as the dew."

"The dewdrops sparkling in the early morning sunlight,

each reflect the full-circled image of the heavenly orb. So each saint will shine resplendent in the complete likeness of the Son of God" (W.E. Vine).

"They are an army of volunteers, priest-warriors, the weapons of whose warfare are not carnal, but beautiful as the dew, constantly being rejuvenated, like the fresh dew every morning, each drop reflecting the sun in miniature" (Max Isaac Reich).

They are described in Revelation 19:14: "The armies which were in heaven followed Him upon white horses, clothed in fine linen, white and clean."

But perhaps the words, "Thou hast the dew of thy youth," could refer to Christ Himself. At His ascension, He went back to heaven at the peak of manhood, thirty-three years old. Two thousand years have not written any furrows on His brow. Forever He will be the perfect Man, while at the same time, King of kings and Lord of lords.

Verse 4 introduces us to the center and climax of the psalm: "The Lord hath sworn, and will not repent, Thou art a priest for ever after the order of Melchizedek." There are only three Scriptures that speak of Melchizedek. In Genesis 14:17-24, we find him historically; in Psalm 110, he is viewed prophetically; and in Hebrews 5-7, doctrinally. The outstanding thing about him was that he was both a king and a priest at the same time. He appears suddenly in the historical record, and, after blessing Abraham in the name of the Most High God, and receiving tithes from him, he disappears just as suddenly. He was a real historical character, but the important factor is that in him royalty and priesthood are combined—these are two offices, that, as far as man is concerned, God has separated.

Uzziah attempted to perform the offices of king and priest and God smote him. He was a leper until the day of his death (2 Chron. 26:16-23). The fact is that God has reserved the priestly miter and the royal diadem to be placed on one head, the head of His well-beloved Son. Zechariah 6:12-13 tells us: "Thus speaketh the Lord of hosts, saying, Behold the man whose name is The BRANCH; and He shall grow up out of His place, and He shall build the temple of the Lord: Even He shall build the temple of the Lord; and He shall bear the glory, and shall sit and rule upon His throne; and He shall be a priest upon His throne: and the counsel of peace shall be between them both."

The first war, recorded in Genesis 14, when Melchizedek appears, is a picture of the final world war, the battle of Armageddon, when Christ shall come as Priest-King and, after subduing His enemies, shall pick up His scepter and reign from sea to sea.

3. AS JUDGE (VV. 5-6)

The second coming of Christ, revealed in the New Testament, is in two stages. First He comes for His bride, the Church (1 Thess. 4:13-18; 1 Cor. 15:51-58). This is the *parousia,* the presence of Christ with His own. Then comes the *bema,* the judgment seat of Christ, the day of Christ in heaven, when rewards will be distributed for faithful service.

At the same time, on earth there will be a time of unparalleled judgment, the day of the Lord, the great tribulation. This will be climaxed by the gathering of the military might of the nations against Jerusalem. The object is to annihilate Israel, to wipe her off the map, to settle the Jewish question once and for all. It will be like vultures surrounding a carcass (Mt. 24:28). The oil of the Middle East and the chemicals of the Dead Sea are perhaps the spoils of war.

The political setup according to Scripture seems to be: a western democracy with headquarters in Rome, headed up by the Man of Sin, the first beast of Revelation 13, in the west. The Northeastern confederacy, Russia and her satellites, in the far reaches of the north. Then the king of the north, the

Arab nations to the immediate north of Israel; the area out of which the Assyrian, the overflowing scourge, arose in Isaiah 28. Then the king of the south, Egypt, and the African nations allied with her. Finally, the kings of the east with an army of two hundred million men. What a tremendous combination of power and military might! At the critical moment, the heavens will open and Christ shall come.

It looks as if the position of Israel is hopeless. "For I will gather all nations against Jerusalem to battle; and the city shall be taken, and the houses rifled, and the women ravished; and half of the city shall go forth into captivity, and the residue of the people shall not be cut off from the city. Then shall the Lord go forth, and fight against those nations, as when He fought in the day of battle. And His feet shall stand in that day upon the mount of Olives, which is before Jerusalem on the east, and the mount of Olives shall cleave in the midst thereof toward the east and toward the west, and there shall be a very great valley; and half of the mountain shall remove toward the north, and half of it toward the south...and the Lord my God shall come, and all the saints with Thee" (Zech. 14:2-5).

Psalm 110:5-6 outlines four mighty blows on His enemies which the Lord will deliver at the battle of Armageddon:

a) "The Lord at Thy right hand shall strike through kings in the day of His wrath." The two outstanding leaders will be the two beasts of Revelation 13. The man of sin, the beast out of the sea, will demand universal worship and will set up his image in the Temple in Jerusalem. The second is his henchman, the false prophet, the leader of the apostate part of the nation of Israel. The first has headquarters in Rome, the second in Jerusalem. Both of these are captured and cast alive into the lake of fire (Rev. 19:19-20).

b) "He shall judge among the heathen" (v. 6). After the battle, the judgment of the living nations takes place (Mt. 25:31-

46). "When the Son of man shall come in His glory, and all the holy angels with Him, then shall He sit upon the throne of His glory: and before Him shall be gathered all nations: and He shall separate them one from another, as a shepherd divideth his sheep from the goats: and He shall set the sheep on His right hand but the goats on the left." They will be judged according to what they did with the messengers who came with the gospel of the kingdom. Those who received them and their message will go into the kingdom, but those who rejected Christ in the person of His servants will go into everlasting punishment.

c) "He shall fill the places with the dead bodies" (v. 6). Ezekiel 38-39 describes an invasion of the land by Gog and Magog, Meshech and Tubal, along with a number of allied powers. They come from the far reaches of the north (Ezek. 38:15). These are usually taken to be Russia and her satellites. They come to take a spoil, and a prey (Ezek. 38:12). But when the Lord deals with them, it will take seven months to bury the dead and seven years to clean up the land (Ezek. 39:9-12; Rev. 19:17-21).

d) "He shall wound the head [singular] over many countries" (v. 6). This is usually applied by commentators to the Man of Sin of 2 Thessalonians 2:3-10, the first beast of Revelation 13. But could it not also be applied to the devil himself, the third member of the unholy trinity, forming this caricature of the Holy Trinity? There is the first beast to whom worship is directed, representing the Father. There is the second beast, the false prophet, the one who comes in his own name, the leader of the apostate part of Israel, the Antichrist, who directs worship to the first beast and who works miracles before him. Behind him is that evil spirit, the devil, who energizes them both. The first two are cast alive into the lake of fire. But the devil is arrested and cast into the abyss where he is confined during the millennium. Genesis 3:15 promises: "I will put enmity between thee and the woman...between thy seed and her seed; it shall bruise thy head, and thou shalt bruise His heel!" Satan's head was bruised at Calvary and, after a final revolt at the end of the millennium, of which he is the leader, he too will be cast into the lake of fire, where the beast and the false prophet are (Rev. 20:7-10).

THE APPENDIX (V. 7)

"He shall drink of the brook in the way: therefore shall He lift up the head." The uplifted head of the conquering Christ is in contrast to the wounded head of verse 6. While on earth in humiliation, He said, "Foxes have holes and birds of the air have nests, but the Son of man hath not where to lay His head" (Lk. 9:58).

The reference to drinking of the brook by the way may be to Gideon's three hundred who lapped water like a dog before they went into battle. Instead of lying flat as they drank, they kept alert and ready to meet the enemy (Jud. 7:5-7).

David may also be thinking of his own experience in the cave of Adullam when, rejected and homesick, he mused aloud, "O that one would give me drink of the water of the well of Bethlehem." Three brave men, without any command, arose from the fire and, buckling on their swords, slipped through the lines of the Philistines, drew the water from the well, and brought it to him. As David looked at these three who had risked their lives for him, he refused to drink it. By that act of devotion, the water had been turned symbolically into blood, and David poured it out as a drink offering before the Lord. But he did not forget that act. Later when he became king and was on the throne, the brave deed was suitably rewarded.

So it is today. By some act of true devotion we have the privilege of giving a refreshing drink to our heavenly David, and one day we will see that Head—once crowned with thorns, lifted up in glory and majesty.

12
Psalm 8
The First and the Last Adam

PSALM 8

To the chief Musician upon Gittith
A Psalm of David

1 O LORD our Lord, how excellent is Thy name in all the earth! who
hast set Thy glory above the heavens.
2 Out of the mouth of babes and sucklings hast Thou ordained
strength because of Thine enemies, that Thou mightest still the
enemy and the avenger.
3 When I consider Thy heavens, the work of Thy fingers, the moon
and the stars, which Thou hast ordained;
4 What is man, that Thou art mindful of him? and the son of man,
that Thou visitest him?
5 For Thou hast made him a little lower than the angels, and hast
crowned him with glory and honor.
6 Thou madest him to have dominion over the works of Thy hands;
Thou hast put all things under his feet:
7 All sheep and oxen, yea, and the beasts of the field;

8 The fowl of the air, and the fish of the sea, and whatsoever passeth through the paths of the seas.
9 O LORD our Lord, how excellent is Thy name in all the earth!

THE FIRST AND THE LAST ADAM

Psalm 8 is quoted four times in the New Testament and each time it is applied to the Lord Jesus.

a) Matthew 21:16: He presents Himself officially at the Temple as the Son of David, and drives out the money merchants; the multitude and the children cried: "Hosanna to the Son of David: Blessed is He that cometh in the name of the Lord; Hosanna in the highest." In reply to the indignant protest of the leaders, He said, "Have ye never read: Out of the mouth of babes and sucklings Thou hast perfected praise?" God is still glorified in the simple faith of little children, and their songs glorifying His name.

b) 1 Corinthians 15:27: In this passage we see the ultimate triumph of the resurrected and glorified Christ, who is declared to be the second Man and the last Adam. "The end" is described in four stages: i) when He shall have put down all rule and all authority and all power. ii) For He must reign; till He hath put all enemies under His feet; the last enemy that shall be destroyed is death. iii) Then the Son also Himself shall be subject unto Him that put all things under Him. iv) That God may be all in all.

c) Ephesians 1:20-22: The ascended Head of the Church, resurrected and enthroned, with all things under His feet, is given Headship of the Church, which is His body and the fullness of Him.

d) Hebrews 2:6-9: This presents Christ as the last Adam, crowned with glory and honor, picking up the crown and scepter which had fallen from the head of the first Adam, and along with His consort, the Church, having dominion and sovereignty over a redeemed creation. What a wealth of teaching, and a galaxy of glories of the risen Christ these passages present to us!

After contemplating God's glory and majesty in the heavens, we are taken back in this psalm to the garden of Eden, and then forward to millennial days when the Messiah will be upon the throne reigning over a restored creation.

Notice first the title. *To the chief Musician upon Gittith, A Psalm of David.* Jewish commentators say the word "Gittith" is derived from "Gath" and is a musical instrument used there. Others interpret the word as meaning "winepress." Dr. Thirtle says the inscription "Muth-labben," heading Psalm 9, really is a subscription to Psalm 8. It means "death of the son" or "death of the champion," i.e., Goliath. If so, it could refer to David's contest with Goliath, a graphic picture of the victory of Christ over Satan in the temptation and at the cross. Where the first Adam fell and lost dominion under Satan's wiles and temptation, the last Adam gloriously overcame.

AN OUTLINE OF PSALM 8

Psalm 8 has four parts:

1. Worship and Witness (vv. 1-2).
2. Wonder of Creation (v. 3).
3. Man in Dominion (vv. 4-8).
4. Worship (v. 9).

1. WORSHIP AND WITNESS (VV. 1-2)

The psalm begins and ends with a doxology in the same words: "O Jehovah our Adonai, how excellent is Thy name in all the earth!" It is completely enclosed in worship and in extolling God's excellent name. Lurking in the background of this worship is the sinister figure of one called "the enemy and the avenger." This no doubt is Satan. He, as the serpent, insinuated himself into the garden of Eden to deceive and destroy God's handiwork.

Here the avenger is not the *goel,* the kinsman-redeemer-avenger, but the *naquam,* the self-avenger (cf., Ps. 44:16). But his mouth is closed by the testimony of babes and sucklings. Gaebelein says that the babes here are newborn souls. That of course is true, but is there anything more delightful than the faith and trust of a little child? Our Lord spoke of it in Matthew 11:25 in His great prayer of thanksgiving: "I thank Thee, O Father, Lord of heaven and earth, because Thou hast hid these things from the wise and prudent, and hast revealed them unto babes. Even so, Father: for so it seemed good in Thy sight."

It is usually the learned and sophisticated that side with the enemy and the avenger by doubt and denial of God's Word. He refers to it again in Matthew 18:1-6: "Except ye be converted, and become as little children, ye shall not enter into the kingdom of heaven." Then in Matthew 21:16, He quotes the passage from the psalm, "Have ye never read, Out of the mouth of babes and sucklings Thou hast perfected praise?" The enemy and the avenger here were the leaders of the nation that rejected His claims.

2. THE WONDER OF CREATION (V. 3)

"When I consider Thy heavens, the work of Thy fingers, the moon and the stars, which Thou hast ordained." God calls man to look up and consider the heavens. Satan encourages man to look down like the beasts of the field that grovel in the mire and dirt. The Greek word for man, *anthropos,* means "one who looks up." The only telescope David had was the telescope of faith. While tending his sheep in the fields of Bethlehem, lying on his back at night beside a fire, he would have plenty of time to look up at the starry skies. Psalm 19 mentions the sun in the daytime, but Psalm 8 describes the moon and the stars at night.

Astronomy puts puny man in his place. Think of the sobering effect on man's ego of the study of the spiral galaxies and the island universes of the Milky Way! These are called the work of His fingers, God's embroidery. The work of His hand and arm is linked with salvation and the security of the believer, as well.

The Bible says that the stars are like the sand of the seashore, innumerable. Skeptics used to laugh at the statement. On a clear night we can count about three thousand with the naked eye, but in these days of radio-astronomy and the Hubble space telescope, all that has been changed. Our minds, although amazing in complexity, cannot comprehend the fathomless immensity of the universe. The star Betelguese in Orion is so large that it is said that our whole solar system—sun, moon, and planets—could describe their orbits inside it. Carlyle spoke of "the silent palace of the Eternal, of which our sun is but the porch lamp!" Our earth is like a grain of sand on a mighty seashore.

3. MAN IN DOMINION (VV. 4-8)

When we consider the immensity and majesty of the universe, it may seem incredible that Almighty God, who has created it, should take any notice of us earth dwellers, never mind visit us. But at the other end of the spectrum is the teeming life in a drop of dirty ditch water, and more amazing still, the invisible controlled power inside the atom. It gives point to David's question: "What is man, that Thou art mindful of him? or the son of man [Ben-Adam], that Thou visitest him?" (Cf., Ps. 144:3-4.) As a result of the fall and the curse, a mosquito or a microbe can put man on his back or into his grave.

The psalmist moves from the smallness and frailty of man

to the greatness which God has conferred upon him through grace. God does three things for frail man:

a) He is mindful of him, in His thoughts and purpose.
b) He visits him in the Incarnation.
c) He sets him over the works of His hands.
d) He crowns him as viceroy on earth.
Here we have man in dignity, dominion, and destiny.

Verses 4-8 look back to Genesis 2 and look forward to Hebrews 2.

Genesis 2: Man was made a little lower than angels. The Hebrew word is *Elohim,* the usual word for God. This is the only place where it is translated angels, and the Epistle to the Hebrews takes it in that sense. Man in innocence was placed as God's viceroy over creation. He was created in the image and likeness of God, and twice was given the command to have dominion. His sovereignty extended over four spheres: domestic animals, the beast of the field, birds of the air, and fish of the sea. In Genesis 2:19-20, he names the animals. Thus in innocence man had four great gifts conferred upon him: sovereignty, a sabbath rest, a spouse, and service. Eden was a perfect environment. He was given a scepter and a crown. Eric Sauer calls him "the king of creation."

But in Genesis 3, all is upset by the Fall and its terrible consequences. The crown has fallen from his head and his scepter is in the dust. The writer of the Hebrews Epistle sadly says: "We see not yet all things put under him." What we do see is a groaning creation under the curse. Man is afraid of the lion and the snake, and even of a dog or a mouse! The first Adam and his posterity have sadly failed in the original mandate that was given to him.

Hebrews 2. The writer introduces the subject of the Head of a new creation and a new family with the words: "But we see Jesus." Here we have the second man, the last Adam. In Hebrews 1, we have a sevenfold statement of His deity, backed by seven quotations from the Old Testament, mostly from the Messianic psalms. In chapter 2, we see a sevenfold glory of the Son of Man, backed by four Messianic prophesies, the principal one being Psalm 8. "The world to come" (v. 5) is a technical expression in Hebrews for the millennium. It has not been made subject to angels. Dominion has not been committed to them. After quoting Psalm 8:4-8, the writer says: "We do not see everything in subjection to him," and then immediately adds: "But we see Jesus, who [for a little while] was made a little lower than the angels, crowned with glory and honor." He outlines four great epoch-making events, fulfilling the prophecy of Psalm 8. Two of these are historic and two are prophetic.

a) *Made for a little time lower than the angels.* Here it is with a view to the suffering of death—all that was involved in His incarnation and crucifixion, His thirty-three years on this planet.

b) *Crowned with glory and honor.* This points to His glorification. For the last two thousand years, He has been sitting in the highest place, on His Father's throne.

c) *Set over the works of thy hands.* This anticipates His coronation, and His rule on earth for one thousand years.

d) *All things under His feet.* This speaks of the consummation, the eternal state when all opposition shall be put down permanently.

The coming power and authority of the Son of Man over creation was demonstrated during His earthly life here below: His dominion over the forces of nature (Mk. 4:39-41; Jn. 2:3-11; 6:5-14); over the wild beasts in the wilderness (Mk. 1:13); over domesticated animals (Lk. 19:30); over the fish of the sea (Mt. 17:27); and over the fowl of the air (Lk. 3:22).

THE TITLE "SON OF MAN" (PS. 8:4; HEB. 2:6)

The title, "Son of Man," first used in Psalm 8:4 and quoted

in Hebrews 2:6, denotes Lordship over the earth, the position from which the first Adam fell—dominion over the earth, sea, and air. The first reference in the Gospels is Matthew 8:20, "The Son of man hath not where to lay His head." It emphasizes His rejection instead of dominion. The title is used 84 times in the Gospels, always by the Lord Himself. It was His claim to the universe. It is vitally linked to His temptation in the wilderness, where the scene in Eden is re-enacted, but where the first Adam failed, He gloriously overcame.

As Son of Man, authority to execute judgment has been committed unto Him (Jn. 5:27). Except in Acts 7:56, at the death of Stephen, and in Hebrews 2:6, the title is not used again until Revelation 1. Its omission from the Epistles is significant. It is the usual title in the apocalyptic judgments in Revelation. The last reference shows Him coming with many diadems on His head, and the sickle and the sword in His hand, to take dominion (Rev. 14:14). Whenever His coming to reign is mentioned, it is the coming of the Son of Man. See Daniel 7:13: "One like unto the Son of Man coming in the clouds of heaven." He is given dominion, glory, and a kingdom. In consequence, among the Jews it was the popular and official title of the Messiah. Ezekiel uses it 93 times of frail, short-lived man in contrast to the Eternal God.

Thus the title is used in Scripture in four senses:

a) The ideal, representative archetypical, pattern Man, the One who conquered where Adam failed (Ps. 8; Heb. 2).

b) The Messiah in prophecy (Dan. 7:13; Rev. 14:14).

c) The incarnate Saviour in His perfect humanity—our Lord's favorite title.

d) The coming King and Judge who assumes world dominion in the millennium.

"All things under His feet." This expression occurs three times in the New Testament, and is applied to our Lord Jesus Christ: In Hebrews 2:5-15 to His being crowned with glory and honor; in Ephesians 1:22, to Christ and His Church; in 1 Corinthians 15:25-27, to His coming in glory.

"The dignity and dominion conferred on man at his creation and crowning could only be entrusted and exercised by a man perfect in character, wisdom, and power. Now in Him, who became the Son of Man, we have found the meeting place of the divinely perfect and the perfectly divine" (William Heron, "Studies in the Psalms," *Believer's Magazine,* 1961, p. 71).

Well, then, might the psalmist repeat the ascription of praise to Jehovah with which he commenced: "O Lord, our Lord, how excellent is Thy name in all the earth!"

13
Psalm 72
The Millennial Reign of the King

PSALM 72

A Psalm for Solomon

1 Give the king Thy judgments, O God, and Thy righteousness unto the king's son.
2 He shall judge Thy people with righteousness, and Thy poor with judgment.
3 The mountains shall bring peace to the people, and the little hills, by righteousness.
4 He shall judge the poor of the people, He shall save the children of the needy, and shall break in pieces the oppressor.
5 They shall fear Thee as long as the sun and moon endure, throughout all generations.
6 He shall come down like rain upon the mown grass: as showers that water the earth.
7 In His days shall the righteous flourish; and abundance of peace so long as the moon endureth.
8 He shall have dominion also from sea to sea, and from the river

unto the ends of the earth.
9 They that dwell in the wilderness shall bow before Him; and His enemies shall lick the dust.
10 The kings of Tarshish and of the isles shall bring presents: the kings of Sheba and Seba shall offer gifts.
11 Yea, all kings shall fall down before Him: all nations shall serve Him.
12 For He shall deliver the needy when he crieth, the poor also, and him that hath no helper.
13 He shall spare the poor and needy, and shall save the souls of the needy.
14 He shall redeem their soul from deceit and violence: and precious shall their blood be in His sight.
15 And He shall live, and to Him shall be given of the gold of Sheba: prayer also shall be made for Him continually; and daily shall He be praised.
16 There shall be an handful of corn in the earth upon the top of the mountains; the fruit thereof shall shake like Lebanon: and they of the city shall flourish like grass of the earth.
17 His name shall endure for ever: His name shall be continued as long as the sun: and men shall be blessed in Him: all nations shall call Him blessed.
18 Blessed be the LORD God, the God of Israel, who only doeth wondrous things.
19 And blessed be His glorious name for ever: and let the whole earth be filled with His glory; Amen, and Amen.
20 The prayers of David the son of Jesse are ended.

THE MILLENNIAL REIGN OF THE KING

The second Book of Psalms, commencing with Psalm 42 and ending with Psalm 72, contains four which are definitely Messianic. Psalm 69, the cross; Psalm 68, the ascension; Psalm 45, the King-Bridegroom; and Psalm 72, the millennial reign.

There are many passages in the Old Testament which predict a time of universal peace and rest for this troubled world. The seventh day of creation, when God rested from His work, and the feast of tabernacles, the last feast in Israel's calendar, refer to it typically. The reigns of David and Solomon over the united twelve tribes of Israel give us a picture of it politically. The Prophet Isaiah, in some of the most beautiful language to be found in any literature, describes it prophetically. There are four passages in his prophecy which deal with it: Isaiah 2; 11; 32-33; and 65-66. The prophecies of Ezekiel, Daniel, and Zechariah also have long sections describing the glories of the kingdom.

There are a number of psalms that speak of the thousand years' reign of the Messiah, viz., 2, 8, 22, 24, 95-100.

In the New Testament, the transfiguration scene recorded in Matthew 17:1-9 and Luke 9:27-36 is a preview of the kingdom glories of the Messiah given to the disciples.

In Revelation 20:1-7, the term "a thousand years" occurs six times. It indicates the period when Satan will be in prison, and when Christ and those who suffered under the persecution of the beast, and had part in the first resurrection, will live and reign with Him a thousand years.

In view of all this accumulated scriptural evidence, it is rather amazing that there are people today, called amillennialists, who would either deny or spiritualize the great truth that the Messiah will literally reign as King in the city of Jerusalem where He was formerly rejected and crucified.

Psalm 72 is not verbally quoted in the New Testament, but actually it gathers up all the details concerning this glorious period and expresses them poetically. It is truly a Messianic psalm, with six themes:

1. The judgment of the King and His Son (Ps. 72:1-7).
2. The universal extent of His kingdom (vv. 8-11).
3. The impartial justice of His reign (vv. 12-15).
4. The effect on nature. The curse removed (v. 16).

5. The fulfillment of the promise to Abraham (vv. 17-19).
6. The answer to David's prayers (v. 20).

1. THE KING'S JUDGMENT (VV. 1-7)

The psalm is "For Solomon." His reign, which is a picture of the millennium, commenced with a judgment on the enemies of the kingdom. Adonijah had rebelled against David his father. Shimei had cursed him at the time of the Absalom rebellion. Joab had no regard for David's feelings and had broken his heart by his brutal killing of Absalom, Abner and Amasa (see 1 Ki. 2:1-9). Solomon's first task was to deal with these men in judgment. This had to be done in a righteous manner. The word "righteousness" is mentioned four times in the first section of the psalm.

Similarly the reign of Messiah will commence with a judgment, first on the united armies surrounding Jerusalem at the battle of Armageddon, and then on the living nations, the survivors of the great tribulation (Mt. 25:31-46). Those who have accepted the messengers and the gospel of the kingdom during tribulation days will go into the kingdom, but those who have rejected it will go into everlasting punishment which was prepared for the devil and his angels.

2. THE EXTENT OF THE KINGDOM (VV. 8-11)

"He shall have dominion also from sea to sea, and from the river unto the ends of the earth. The kings of Tarshish and of the isles shall bring presents…the kings of Sheba and Seba shall offer gifts."

During the millennium, Jerusalem will be the world's metropolis. Tarshish would be the farthest point west, and Sheba and Seba the farthest east known to the ancients. "The isles" in Scripture seems to mean the western coast lands of Europe (1 Ki. 10:22). The land promised to Abraham in Genesis 15:18 was "from the river of Egypt unto the great river, the river Euphrates." That would take in Lebanon, Syria, Iran, Iraq, and Saudi Arabia: "From sea to sea, and from the river unto the ends of the earth" would be from the Mediterranean to the Persian Gulf and from the Nile to the Euphrates. The borders of Immanuel's land during the millennium are outlined in Ezekiel 47:13-23, but the dominion of the Messiah will take in the whole world, north, south, east, and west. All will come under His righteous but benevolent administration. Communications will be rapid and secure.

The parable of the pounds in Luke 19:11-27 teaches us that those who have been faithful in the trust committed to them in this church age, will be given positions of administration in the kingdom.

3. THE IMPARTIAL JUSTICE OF HIS REIGN (VV. 12-15)

"For He shall deliver the needy when he crieth, the poor also, and him that hath no helper…He shall redeem their soul from deceit and violence: and precious shall their blood be in His sight."

The four world empires in the times of the Gentiles have all been founded by bloodshed and violence. After they were established, they were characterized by oppression, slavery, and infanticide. But in the administration of the Messiah there will be no bribery, corruption, or miscarriage of justice. The One upon the throne is the perfect embodiment of wisdom, love, and power.

4. THE EFFECT ON NATURE: THE CURSE REMOVED (V. 16)

"There shall be an handful of corn in the earth, on the top of the mountains; the fruit thereof shall shake like Lebanon." The mountain top is usually rocky and barren, but here it is like a fruitful field. As a result of the Fall and the curse, thorns and thistles, weeds and pests, the farmer has to wrestle against the forces of nature to get a crop and eke out his living. But that will all be changed. "The wilderness and the solitary place shall be glad for them; and the desert shall rejoice, and blossom as the rose. It shall blossom abundantly, and rejoice even with joy and singing: the glory of Lebanon shall be given unto it, the excellency of Carmel and Sharon, they shall see the glory of the Lord, and the excellency of our God" (Isa. 35:1-2).

"The wolf also shall dwell with the lamb, and the leopard shall lie down with the kid; and the calf and the young lion and the fatling together; and a little child shall lead them. And the cow and the bear shall feed; their young ones shall lie down together; and the lion shall eat straw like the ox. And the sucking child shall play on the hole of the asp, and the weaned child shall put his hand on the cockatrice' den. They shall not hurt nor destroy in all My holy mountain: for the earth shall be full of the knowledge of the Lord, as the waters cover the sea" (Isa. 11:6-9).

Creation's groan and travail (Rom. 8:18-22) will be exchanged for a song of praise at the manifestation of the sons of God.

5. The Fulfillment of the Promise to Abraham (vv. 17-19)

When the Lord appeared to Abraham in Genesis 12, He gave him a sevenfold promise, the final clause of which is: "In thee shall all families of the earth be blessed." He was promised a threefold seed—as the dust of the earth, as the stars of heaven, and as the sand of the seashore. He has an earthly seed, the people of Israel; a heavenly, those who have a similar faith to his, the Church; and through him, all the nations of the earth. Paul points out in Galatians 3:16 that the word "seed" is singular and is all headed up in one seed, which is Christ. Every blessing to either Jew or Gentile or to the Church of God has its source and outcome in that One who suffered on the cross and who will be the King-Priest on His throne.

6. THE ANSWER TO DAVID'S PRAYERS (V. 20)

"The concluding verse is important. That purpose of God, of which the Church is the object, was no part of divine revelation to David. A glorified Christ, reigning over Israel and the nations of the world, filled the compass of his hope as a receiver of promise and a prophet of God. His prayers were ended in the utterance of that desire. Of heavenly things, as they are now revealed in the Church by the Spirit, he had no knowledge. As a master and prophet in Israel, he spoke of earthly things, and his soul entered into them as the proper objects of his hope and desire" (A. Pridham).

David was a man of prayer. Again and again in the varied experiences and crises of life, he "inquired of the Lord." This is one of the outstanding differences between him and Saul. But now his prayers are ended with this magnificent vision of the millennium when David's Son and David's Lord will be on the throne. And He will never be deposed or replaced.

14
Psalm 89
The Davidic Covenant

PSALM 89

Maschil of Ethan the Ezrahite

1 I will sing of the mercies of the LORD for ever: with my mouth
will I make known Thy faithfulness to all generations.
2 For I have said, Mercy shall be built up for ever: Thy faithfulness
shalt Thou establish in the very heavens.
3 I have made a covenant with My chosen, I have sworn unto David
My servant,
4 Thy seed will I establish for ever, and build up thy throne to all
generations. Selah.
5 And the heavens shall praise Thy wonders, O LORD: Thy faithful-
ness also in the congregation of the saints.
6 For who in the heaven can be compared unto the LORD? who
among the sons of the mighty can be likened unto the LORD?
7 God is greatly to be feared in the assembly of the saints, and to be
had in reverence of all them that are about Him.
8 O LORD God of hosts, who is a strong LORD like unto Thee? or to

Thy faithfulness round about Thee?
9 Thou rulest the raging of the sea: when the waves thereof arise, Thou stillest them.
10 Thou hast broken Rahab in pieces, as one that is slain; Thou hast scattered Thine enemies with Thy strong arm.
11 The heavens are Thine, the earth also is Thine: as for the world and the fulness thereof, Thou hast founded them.
12 The north and the south Thou hast created them: Tabor and Hermon shall rejoice in Thy name.
13 Thou hast a mighty arm: strong is Thy hand,and high is Thy right hand.
14 Justice and judgment are the habitation of Thy throne: mercy and truth shall go before Thy face.
15 Blessed is the people that know the joyful sound: they shall walk, O LORD, in the light of Thy countenance .
16 In Thy name shall they rejoice all the day: and in Thy righteousness shall they be exalted.
17 For Thou art the glory of their strength: and in Thy favor our horn shall be exalted.
18 For the LORD is our defense; and the Holy One of Israel is our King.
19 Then thou spakest in vision to Thy holy one, and saidst, I have laid help upon one that is mighty; I have exalted one chosen out of the people.
20 I have found David My servant; with My holy oil have I anointed him:
21 With whom My hand shall be established: Mine arm also shall strengthen him.
22 The enemy shall not exact upon him; nor the son of wickedness afflict him.
23 And I will beat down his foes before his face, and plague them that hate him.
24 But My faithfulness and My mercy shall be with him: and in My name shall his horn be exalted.
25 I will set his hand also in the sea, and his right hand in the rivers.

26 He shall cry unto Me, Thou art my father, my God, and the rock of my salvation.
27 Also I will make Him My firstborn, higher than the kings of the earth.
28 My mercy will I keep for Him for evermore, and My covenant shall stand fast with Him.
29 His seed also will I make to endure for ever, and His throne as the days of heaven.
30 If his children forsake My law, and walk not in My judgments;
31 If they break My statutes, and keep not My commandments;
32 Then will I visit their transgression with the rod, and their iniquity with stripes.
33 Nevertheless My loving-kindness will I not utterly take from him, nor suffer My faithfulness to fail.
34 My covenant will I not break, nor alter the thing that is gone out of My lips.
35 Once have I sworn by My holiness that I will not lie unto David.
36 His seed shall endure for ever, and his throne as the sun before Me.
37 It shall be established for ever as the moon, and as a faithful witness in heaven. Selah.
38 But Thou hast cast off and abhorred, Thou hast been wroth with Thine anointed.
39 Thou hast made void the covenant of Thy servant: Thou hast profaned his crown by casting it to the ground.
40 Thou hast broken down all his hedges; Thou hast brought his strongholds to ruin.
41 All that pass by the way spoil him: he is a reproach to his neighbors.
42 Thou hast set up the right hand of his adversaries; Thou hast made all his enemies to rejoice.
43 Thou hast also turned the edge of his sword, and hast not made him to stand in the battle.
44 Thou hast made his glory to cease, and cast his throne down to the ground.

45 The days of his youth hast Thou shortened: Thou hast covered him with shame. Selah.
46 How long, LORD? wilt Thou hide Thyself for ever? shall Thy wrath burn like fire?
47 Remember how short my time is: wherefore hast Thou made all men in vain?
48 What man is he that liveth, and shall not see death? shall he deliver his soul from the hand of the grave? Selah.
49 Lord, where are Thy former loving-kindnesses, which Thou swarest unto David in Thy truth?
50 Remember, Lord, the reproach of Thy servants; how I do bear in my bosom the reproach of all the mighty people;
51 Wherewith Thine enemies have reproached, O LORD; wherewith they have reproached the footsteps of Thine anointed.
52 Blessed be the LORD for evermore. Amen, and Amen.

THE DAVIDIC COVENANT

The author of the psalm is Ethan the Ezrahite. His other name was Jeduthun (see 1 Chron. 25 and 16:41-42). He was one of Solomon's wisest councilors (1 Ki. 4:31). He must have known what God said to Solomon about his sin and idolatry and how the kingdom would be taken from his son (1 Ki. 11:9-13). This throws light on his impassioned appeal to Jehovah in the latter part of the psalm. It is possible that Ethan outlived Solomon and saw the breakup of the kingdom that he describes.

AN OUTLINE OF PSALM 89

The psalm is in two main parts:

1. The Davidic Covenant, based on God's faithfulness (vv. 1-37).

2. Its present failure, but future fulfillment (vv. 38-52). It is a *maschil* psalm. The word means teaching or instruction.

1. THE DAVIDIC COVENANT (VV. 1-37)

The covenants which God made with His people is one of the major themes of Holy Scripture. Four of them are related to the nation of Israel:

a) *The covenant made with Abraham* (Gen. 15). This had to do with a seed and a land.

b) *The covenant made at Sinai* with the people of Israel, now redeemed from slavery in Egypt. Here the nation was born. The Law and a place of worship, the Tabernacle, were committed to them (Ex. 19).

c) *The Palestinian covenant* was a warning against idolatry and departure, and a promise of ultimate restoration to the land (Deut. 28-30).

d) *The covenant made to David* was the promise of a kingdom, a dynasty, and a throne given to him and his posterity in perpetuity (2 Sam. 7:8-17).

Psalm 89 is occupied principally with the covenant made to David and his seed. In verses 3-4, it is mentioned concisely, but in verses 19-37, it is expanded and expounded. It is based on two of God's attributes, His faithfulness and His loving-kindness. Each of these attributes is mentioned seven times. The first takes us back into the past and the second looks forward into the future.

In the life of David, there is very much failure and sin, as there is among the people of God today, but we too can testify to the faithfulness and loving-kindness and mercy of our God in spite of all our waywardness and sin.

In the extended exposition of the covenant, there is a very precious reference to the Messiah who comes from David's line. "Also I will make Him My firstborn, higher than the kings of the earth. My mercy will I keep for Him for evermore, and My covenant shall stand fast with Him. His seed also will I make to endure for ever, and His throne as the days of heaven" (vv. 27-29).

The "firstborn" is a title that can refer only to Christ. Paul uses it in connection with creation and redemption. In stating the glory of Christ in His deity, he says, "Who is the image of the invisible God, the firstborn of every creature. For by Him were all things created, that are in heaven, and that are in earth, visible and invisible, whether they be thrones, or dominions, or principalities, or powers: all things were created by Him, and for Him. And He is before all things, and by Him all things consist. And He is the head of the body, the church; who is the beginning, the firstborn from the dead; that in all things He might have the preeminence. For it pleased the Father that in Him should all fulness dwell" (Col. 1:15-19). Note the twofold use of the term: firstborn in creation and firstborn in resurrection. He is not a creature but the Creator and also the Redeemer. The term is used again in Revelation 1:5: "Jesus Christ, who is the faithful witness, and the first begotten [from among] the dead, and the prince of the kings of the earth."

He is also "higher than the kings of the earth." This can refer only to Immanuel (Isa. 7:13-15; 9:6-7; Micah 5:2).

There is a warning in verses 30-32 concerning David's seed: "If his children [break] My law, and walk not in My judgments; If they break My statutes, and keep not My commandments; then will I visit their transgression with the rod, and their iniquity with stripes." History records how this has been fulfilled to the letter. The seventy years' captivity in Babylon, their subsequent scattering to the ends of the earth, and their suffering at the hands of their enemies, bear eloquent testimony to the truth of the prophecy.

But the covenant stands and is irrevocable. "My covenant will I not break, nor alter the thing that is gone out of My lips. Once have I sworn by My holiness that I will not lie unto David. His seed shall endure for ever, and his throne as the sun before Me. It shall be established for ever as the moon, and as a faithful witness in heaven."

2. ITS PRESENT FAILURE, BUT FINAL FULFILLMENT (VV. 38-52)

In verse 38, there comes a sudden and dramatic change. The song of praise and the note of hope and assurance are turned into despair and hopelessness. What is the reason? The writer speaks of the fences being broken down and the strongholds being laid in ruins. The crown has fallen from his head and lies in the dust; his throne has been cast to the ground.

We, today, from our vantage ground of being able to look back over past history, know the reason for the language of despair in the latter part of the psalm. The orthodox Jew, moaning and knocking his head against the Wailing Wall, is a picture of Israel in unbelief today. When the Son of David was born in Bethlehem, the house of David was represented by a pious maiden and a humble workman, the virgin Mary and Joseph. He was born, not in a palace on Mount Zion, David's ancient citadel and stronghold, but in a stable, and He was cradled in a manger. When He presented Himself to the nation as the Messiah, the Son of David, and the fulfiller of the covenant promise, He was scornfully rejected and crucified. Forty years later, the city and the Temple were reduced to rubble and the people scattered. Truly the fences were down and the stronghold in ruins.

But God has not forgotten His covenant promise. Two thousand years have passed since David's Son and Lord was crucified and raised from the dead. But in God's reckoning a thousand years are as one day. There is a remarkable passage in Hosea 6:1-3: "Come, and let us return unto the Lord: for He hath torn. and He will heal us, He hath smitten, and He will bind us up. After two days will He revive us: in the third day He will raise us up, and we shall live in His sight. Then shall we know, if we follow on to know the Lord: His going forth is prepared as the morning; and He shall come unto us as the rain, as the latter and former rain upon the earth."

When we consider the condition of Israel today, back in the land in unbelief, we wonder whether the third day of the prophecy is about to dawn. God has certainly chastened the seed of Israel with the rod, and more dark days lie ahead in the time of Jacob's trouble, but we can rest assured that the covenant with David has not been abrogated or forgotten in God's purpose. In His own good time it will be fulfilled, and the throne and the crown and the kingdom will be restored to their rightful place. But the One who will occupy the throne and wear the crown will be David's Son and Lord, the First-born, higher than the kings of the earth. The darkness will merge into dawn and the last words of the psalm will be fulfilled: "Blessed be the Lord for evermore. Amen, and Amen!"

15
Psalm 102
The Unchangeable One

PSALM 102

A Prayer of the afflicted, when he is overwhelmed,
and poureth out his complaint before the LORD

1 Hear my prayer, O LORD, and let my cry come unto Thee.
2 Hide not Thy face from me in the day when I am in trouble; incline
Thine ear unto me: in the day when I call answer me speedily.
3 For my days are consumed like smoke, and my bones are burned
as an hearth.
4 My heart is smitten, and withered like grass; so that I forget to eat
my bread.
5 By reason of the voice of my groaning my bones cleave to my skin.
6 I am like a pelican of the wilderness: I am like an owl of the desert.
7 I watch, and am as a sparrow alone upon the house top.
8 Mine enemies reproach me all the day; and they that are mad
against me are sworn against me.
9 For I have eaten ashes like bread, and mingled my drink with
weeping,

10 Because of Thine indignation and Thy wrath: for Thou hast lifted
me up, and cast me down.
11 My days are like a shadow that declineth; and I am withered like
grass.
12 But Thou, O LORD, shalt endure for ever; and Thy remembrance
unto all generations.
13 Thou shalt arise, and have mercy upon Zion: for the time to
favour her, yea, the set time, is come.
14 For Thy servants take pleasure in her stones, and favour the dust
thereof.
15 So the heathen shall fear the name of the LORD, and all the kings
of the earth Thy glory.
16 When the LORD shall build up Zion, He shall appear in His
glory.
17 He will regard the prayer of the destitute, and not despise their
prayer.
18 This shall be written for the generation to come: and the people
which shall be created shall praise the LORD.
19 For He hath looked down from the height of His sanctuary; from
heaven did the LORD behold the earth;
20 To hear the groaning of the prisoner; to loose those that are ap-
pointed to death;
21 To declare the name of the LORD in Zion, and His praise in
Jerusalem;
22 When the people are gathered together, and the kingdoms, to
serve the LORD.
23 He weakened my strength in the way; He shortened my days.
24 I said, O my God, take me not away in the midst of my days; Thy
years are throughout all generations.
25 Of old hast Thou laid the foundation of the earth: and the heav-
ens are the work of Thy hands.
26 They shall perish, but Thou shalt endure: yea, all of them shall
wax old like a garment; as a vesture shalt Thou change them, and
they shall be changed.
27 But Thou art the same, and Thy years shall have no end.

28 The children of Thy servants shall continue, and their seed shall be established before Thee.

THE UNCHANGEABLE ONE

Hebrews 1:10-12 is our authority for regarding Psalm 102 as Messianic. "And Thou, Lord, in the beginning hast laid the foundation of the earth; and the heavens are the works of Thine hands: they shall perish; but Thou remainest; and they all shall wax old as doth a garment; And as a vesture shalt Thou fold them up, and they shall be changed: but Thou art the same, and Thy years shall not fail." These words, addressed to God's beloved Son, are a quotation from Psalm 102 (vv. 25-27). But the title of the psalm, "A Prayer of the afflicted, when he is overwhelmed, and poureth out his complaint before the LORD," is in complete contrast to the last stanza. In the title and the first part of the psalm we see the lonely Man of Sorrows, but in the latter part the immutable, unchanging, Eternal God!

The psalm falls into two parts:

1. The prayer of the rejected and lonely Man (vv. 1-24).
2. Almighty God's answer to the Eternal Son (vv. 25-28).

1. THE PRAYER OF THE REJECTED AND LONELY MAN (VV. 1-24)

There are three main subjects in His prayer:

a) *His lament.* It is a dialogue between the Father and the Son. It has been suggested that the scene of this dialogue is in the garden of Gethsemane. Hebrews 5:7-8 tells us: "Who in the days of His flesh, when He had offered up prayers and supplications with strong crying and tears unto Him who was able to save Him from death, and was heard in that He feared; though He were a Son, yet learned He obedience by the things which He suffered." We cannot probe the depths of that agony in which He sweat as it were great drops of blood falling down to the ground. But it was a personal, intimate transaction between Him and His Father. In the first eleven verses there are 28 personal pronouns. He uses the words "I am" five times.

b) *His loneliness.* He uses three illustrations: "I am like a pelican of the wilderness: I am like an owl of the desert. I watch, and am as a sparrow alone upon the housetop" (vv. 6-7). The pelican is a perfect picture of doleful misery. It sits on the edge of a swamp with its head upon its breast. In Israel it is found only around Lake Huleh. Thompson, in *The Land and the Book,* says: "It is the most sombre, austere bird I ever saw."

This doleful sight is followed by the owl. Its melancholy hoot is heard among ruined buildings. (The word "desert" should be "ruined palaces.") Moping in the ruins and sitting among fallen buildings and graveyards, it is a picture of the mourner. The sparrow is a social bird, but when it loses its mate, it is a mute picture of desolation. All three are emblems of utter abandonment and loneliness. One can be lonely in a crowd; even a big city can be the loneliest place on earth.

The loneliness of Christ in His life here on earth is emphasized in the Gospels in at least four contexts:

i) *His home life.* He had at least four brothers and two sisters (Mk. 6:3). How significant are the words: "For neither did His brethren believe in Him" (Jn. 7:5). Then there are the prophetic words of Psalm 69:8: "I am become a stranger unto My brethren, and an alien unto My mother's children." Apparently it was only after His resurrection that they came to have saving faith (Acts 1:14)

ii) *His prayer life.* On many occasions He went out to a desert place alone to pray. This is emphasized in Mark's Gospel (1:35; 6:46; 14:32). On at least two occasions He spent a whole night in prayer alone: before He chose the twelve apostles (Lk. 6:12), and after the murder of John the Baptist (Mt. 14:23). His times of sacred communion with His Father were spent alone.

iii) *In Gethsemane.* In the garden, He and the disciples were divided into three groups. First eight disciples; then three—Peter and James and John. But He went further, withdrawing from them about a stone's cast (Lk. 22:41) and kneeled down and prayed. He was alone in His agony.

iv) *On the cross.* In the upper room, He had told the disciples: "Ye shall be scattered…and shall leave Me alone, and yet I am not alone, because the Father is with Me" (see also, Jn. 16:32; 8:16, 29). Now Judas had betrayed Him, Peter had denied Him, and the others had forsaken Him and fled. But the cross was the ultimate. When He was crucified, His first words were: "Father, forgive them; for they know not what they do." At the end, He said: "Father, into Thy hands I commend My spirit." But amid the darkness, He cried: "My God, My God, why hast Thou forsaken Me?" He was alone in His vicarious atoning suffering on the tree.

c) *His lifespan.* He uses three similes of the shortness of human life: smoke (v. 3); grass (vv. 4, 11); a shadow that declines (v. 11). Then (v. 24) He prays: "O My God, take Me not away in the midst of My days." The answer to this is: "Thy years shall have no end" (v. 27).

The prayer and its answer remind us so vividly of two passages in the Old Testament: "And after threescore and two weeks shall Messiah be cut off, but not for Himself" (Dan. 9:26); and "who shall declare His generation? for He was cut off out of the land of the living: for the transgression of my people was He stricken" (Isa. 53:8). But here again we have the promise: "He shall see His seed, He shall prolong His days, and the pleasure of the Lord shall prosper in His hand" (v. 10). His life, instead of being extended to the normal seventy years (Ps. 90:10), was cut short in the midst at thirty-three. The reply of His Father emphasizes His eternity in comparison with the world's vanishing dream, which to us seems so solid and enduring.

2. ALMIGHTY GOD'S ANSWER TO THE ETERNAL SON (VV. 25-28)

"Of old hast Thou laid the foundation of the earth: and the heavens are the work of Thy hands. They shall perish, but Thou shalt endure; yea, all of them shall wax old like a garment; as a vesture shalt Thou change them, and they shall be changed: *But Thou art the same,* and Thy years shall have no end."

These are the majestic words, quoted and applied to our Lord in Hebrews 1:10-12. They are in complete contrast to the lonely and forsaken Man, cut off in the midst of His days in the first part of the psalm.

As we look at God's marvelous creation in the heavens and the earth, everything seems so permanent and enduring. Generations of men come and go. Man's little lifespan is so short in comparison with the light years of the stars and the galaxies of the Milky Way. Some of the trees, like the giant sequoias of California, live for more than a thousand years, but then they too die. The mountains and the oceans go on and on, and it would seem that they will be here forever. But not so! The Word of God declares that they too are getting old, like a tattered garment, and one day will be discarded and changed.

This, we are told, agrees with modern science. According to the second law of thermodynamics (entropy), everything in the universe is rapidly winding down. The sun is burning up astronomical tons of matter every second, and it is only a question of time before it burns itself out and becomes cold and dead. The planet on which we live is gradually being denuded of its resources by an exploding population. Coal, oil, and the forests are being used up at an ever-increasing tempo. The rivers, lakes, and oceans are being polluted by chemicals and industry, and even the air and atmosphere which sustain life are being invaded by man's ugly inventions.

The garment is becoming more and more ragged and threadbare. But the Bible declares that one day there will be new heavens and a new earth where righteousness and order will dwell (Isa. 65:17; Rev. 21:1).

In a remarkable passage, the Apostle Peter describes how this will happen: "But the day of the Lord will come as a thief in the night; in the which the heavens shall pass away with a great noise, and the elements shall melt with fervent heat, the earth also and the works that are within shall be burned up. Seeing then that all these things shall be dissolved, what manner of persons ought ye to be in all holy conversation and godliness. Looking for and hasting unto the coming of the day of God, wherein the heavens being on fire shall be dissolved, and the elements shall melt with fervent heat? Nevertheless we, according to His promise, look for new heavens and a new earth, wherein dwelleth righteousness" (2 Pet. 3:10-13).

In contrast to an expiring world, the Eternal God addresses the Eternal Son: "But Thou art the same, and Thy years shall have no end."

One of the titles of the Messiah in Isaiah 9:6 is: "The Father of Eternity." In eternity past, He was the Eternal Son, subsisting in the form of God (Phil. 2:6). In eternity future, as the Kinsman-Redeemer, with His blood-bought consort by His side, He will still be the Eternal Son of the Father. One of the attributes of deity is immutability. "Thou art the same." "Jesus Christ, the same yesterday, and today and for ever" (Heb. 13:8). We add our prayer to the hymn writer's:

> *"Change and decay in all around I see,*
> *O Thou who changest not, abide with me!"*

16
Psalm 118
The Conclusion of the Hallel

PSALM 118

1 O give thanks unto the LORD; for He is good: because His mercy
endureth for ever.
2 Let Israel now say, that His mercy endureth for ever.
3 Let the house of Aaron now say, that His mercy endureth for ever.
4 Let them now that fear the LORD say, that His mercy endureth for
ever.
5 I called upon the LORD in distress: the LORD answered me, and
set me in a large place.
6 The LORD is on my side; I will not fear: what can man do unto
me?
7 The LORD taketh my part with them that help me: therefore shall I
see my desire upon them that hate me.
8 It is better to trust in the LORD than to put confidence in man.
9 It is better to trust in the LORD than to put confidence in princes.
10 All nations compassed me about: but in the name of the LORD

will I destroy them.
11 They compassed me about; yea, they compassed me about: but in
the name of the LORD I will destroy them.
12 They compassed me about like bees; they are quenched as the fire
of thorns: for in the name of the LORD I will destroy them.
13 Thou hast thrust sore at me that I might fall: but the LORD
helped me.
14 The LORD is my strength and song, and is become my salvation.
15 The voice of rejoicing and salvation is in the tabernacles of the
righteous: the right hand of the LORD doeth valiantly.
16 The right hand of the LORD is exalted: the right hand of the
LORD doeth valiantly.
17 I shall not die, but live, and declare the works of the LORD.
18 The LORD hath chastened me sore: but He hath not given me
over unto death.
19 Open to me the gates of righteousness: I will go into them, and I
will praise the LORD:
20 This gate of the LORD, into which the righteous shall enter.
21 I will praise Thee: for Thou hast heard me, and art become my
salvation.
22 The stone which the builders refused is become the head stone of
the corner.
23 This is the LORD's doing; it is marvelous in our eyes.
24 This is the day which the LORD hath made; we will rejoice and
be glad in it.
25 Save now, I beseech Thee, O LORD: O LORD, I beseech Thee,
send now prosperity.
26 Blessed be He that cometh in the name of the LORD: we have
blessed you out of the house of the LORD.
27 God is the LORD, which hath showed us light: bind the sacrifice
with cords, even unto the horns of the altar.
28 Thou art my God, and I will praise Thee: Thou art my God, I will
exalt Thee.
29 O give thanks unto the LORD; for He is good: for His mercy en-
dureth for ever.

THE CONCLUSION OF THE HALLEL

This is the final Messianic psalm. It sums up the teaching in all the others, outlining the history of anti-Semitic persecution throughout the ages, ending with the coming of the Messiah to set up His kingdom. The psalm begins and ends with the same words, an ascription of praise to God: "O give thanks unto the Lord; for He is good: for His mercy endureth for ever."

It is also the final song of the Egyptian hallel, so called because it celebrates the deliverance from Egypt (Ps. 114:1). The hallel consists of six psalms, 113—118 . David Baron, the Hebrew-Christian commentator, says they were sung at the three great feasts, the Passover, Pentecost, and Tabernacles. At the Passover, Psalms 113 and 114 were sung before the drinking of the second cup, and the other four (115 - 118) after the drinking of the fourth cup, at the end of the ceremony. It is very likely that this was the hymn sung by our Lord and His disciples after the institution of the Lord's Supper (Mt. 26:30).

It is the only time in the historical records in the Gospels where we find our Lord singing. In Matthew we find Him preaching and teaching; in Mark He is serving; and in Luke we see Him praying; but here only do we have Him singing. It is intensely interesting to study carefully the words and sentiments in the concluding paragraph of this psalm. It gives us an insight into the thoughts in the mind and heart of our Lord just before He went out of the lighted upper room to Gethsemane and the cross.

The psalm must have been very much in the mind of the Saviour in the last week of His public ministry. It is referred to four times:

a) *At His public presentation at the Temple.* While He was rejected by the nation as a whole, the children sang, "Hosanna to the son of David" (Mt. 21:9; Zech. 9:9).

b) In the parable of the vineyard, He quotes verses 22-23 of the psalm, concerning the rejected stone (Mt. 21:42).

c) In His lament over Jerusalem, He cries: "Ye shall not see Me henceforth, till ye shall say, Blessed is He that cometh in the name of the Lord" (Mt. 23:39).

d) Here, in the singing of the hymn at the Lord's Supper, almost certainly the closing words of the hallel.

The psalm is also quoted by Peter in Acts 4:11 and 1 Peter 2:7; and by Paul in Ephesians 2:20, sealing our authority for calling it a Messianic psalm.

AN OUTLINE OF PSALM 118

The psalm is in three parts:

1. Three groups are called to praise God (vv. 1-4).
2. An historical outline of Israel's suffering through the centuries, climaxed by the great tribulation (vv. 5-18).
3. Final deliverance by Messiah's appearing (vv. 19-29).

1. THREE GROUPS CALLED TO PRAISE THE LORD (V. 1-4)

The three groups mentioned are: Israel, the house of Aaron, and them that fear the Lord. Israel—the people as a whole; the house of Aaron—the priesthood; and them that fear the Lord—the godly remnant (Mal. 3:16).

The Prophets Isaiah and Ezekiel mention the same three groups. They are linked together twice in Psalm 115 and in each case exhorted to trust in the Lord, for He is their help and their shield (vv. 9-13). In every age the people of God could be classified in this way; the people in the aggregate, the leaders, and an inner core of dedicated ones who are the backbone of the testimony. How good it is when all can unite in saying: "His mercy endureth for ever!" The remnant in this case would be those who hold fast to the Messianic hope.

2. AN HISTORICAL OUTLINE OF ISRAEL'S SUFFERING (VV. 5-18)

The history of anti-Semitism, the concerted effort to wipe out the Jew, is a long, sad, and tragic one. It is the conflict of the ages, the battle of the seeds. The seed of the woman and the seed of the serpent have been at daggers drawn from time immemorial, and it will last till the end of time. Pharaoh, Amalek, Athaliah, Nebuchadnezzar, Haman, Antiochus Epiphanes, Herod the Great, the Caesars, Hitler, and Stalin have all had their part in the infamous story. Now it is the Arab world, with billions in oil wealth, which has joined in the cry: "Death to the Jew!" Pagan Rome, and then papal Rome at the Inquisition, as well as Russian pogroms, the gas ovens in the extermination camps of Europe, and the Nuremberg trials, have all piled up the evidence that Satan has employed every known tactic to exterminate the seed of Jacob.

And the story is not complete. Dark days lie ahead for Israel. What has happened in the past will happen again in intensified form during the time of Jacob's trouble (Jer. 30:7). The siege of Jerusalem in AD 70 was just a little foretaste of what will happen at the end. Israel will be surrounded again by her enemies, and on the verge of extermination when, at the critical moment, the heavens will open, and the Messiah will come for their deliverance.

The Gentile nations have not yet learned the lesson of history, that Israel is the apple of God's eye, His chosen people. Those that attack them are attacking God in a very sensitive area, and will reap swift judgment. Hitler learned that when it was too late! When Britain protected and helped the Jew, she rose to greatness and became an empire on which the sun never set. But when she changed her policy, and British soldiers with bayonets drawn turned back the tortured remnant of Israel, fleeing from the ghettos of Europe to the promised land, and sent them to concentration camps in Cyprus, the future for England became dark and bleak. Inside of a generation, she has deteriorated into a third-rate power, riddled with anarchy and economic chaos.

This is the teaching of Psalm 118. Four times in verses 10-12 we have the words: "All nations compassed me about." "They compassed me about like bees." The final fulfillment of this passage will be at Armageddon. The stage is being set in modern times for this ultimate encirclement of the nation, but it will result in the total defeat of the forces of evil by the rider on the white horse, the Messiah.

"It is better to trust in the Lord than to put confidence in princes" (verses 8-9). These verses are said to be the central words in the Bible. In former days, Israel turned to Egypt and Assyria for help, only to be let down. In modern times, it was Britain and the Balfour Declaration. The arm of flesh has always been a broken reed. In contrast, "the right hand of the Lord" is mentioned three times in verses 15-16. In verse 6, Israel can say, "The Lord is on my side; I will not fear: what can man do unto me?" This is the important factor. The Lord is not on the side of the big battalions with unlimited armaments and resources, but on the side of those who put their faith and implicit trust in Him. "The Lord is my strength and my song, and is become my salvation" (v. 14) is a quotation from the song of deliverance at the Red Sea (Ex. 15:2), and is quoted by Isaiah in his exquisite little song of millennial triumph in Isaiah 12:2.

The section closes with a note of victory: "I shall not die, but live, and declare the works of the Lord" (v. 17). "The Lord hath chastened me sore [in the great tribulation]: but He hath not given me over unto death." Present-day events on the political scene in the Middle East vividly illustrate all this!

3. Final Deliverance by the Appearing of Messiah (vv. 19-29)

This section has been called "a precious Messianic jewel." On the last three or four days before Calvary, the mind of our

Lord seemed to dwell on this great passage, as He girded Himself for Gethsemane, Gabbatha, and Golgotha. There are seven significant items:

The opened gates of the city and the Temple (vv. 19-21 cf., Ps. 24).

The rejected stone, made the head of the corner (vv. 22-23).

The day which the Lord made (v. 24), the Day of Atonement.

Hosanna, blessed be He that cometh in the name of the Lord (vv. 25-26).

National conversion (v. 27).

The festal sacrifice (v. 27), the Feast of Tabernacles.

The final benediction (vv. 28-29).

THE OPENED GATES OF THE CITY AND THE TEMPLE (V. 19)

On that tragic day in Passion Week when our Lord presented Himself at the Temple, riding upon an ass' colt (Mt. 21:2-10), He fulfilled the prophetic Scripture in Zechariah 9:9. The incident is recorded in all four Gospels. Sir Robert Anderson has calculated that this took place on the last day of Daniel's sixty-ninth week. This points up the importance of the official presentation of the King to the nation at the Temple. But we know He was rejected, and as He sadly left the Temple and the city He said: "Behold, your house is left unto you desolate." *Ichabod* (abandoned) was written over it.

But in a coming day, the gates of both the city and the Temple will be thrown open to the mighty Conqueror and He will occupy the hill and the house. Then they will be the gates of righteousness (Ps. 24:7-10). "Lift up your heads, O ye gates... even lift them up, ye everlasting doors; and the King of glory shall come in."

THE REJECTED STONE, THE HEAD OF THE CORNER (V. 22)

"The stone which the builders refused is become the head

stone of the corner. This is the Lord's doing; it is marvelous in our eyes." There are four other references to the Stone in the Old Testament: Genesis 49:24; Isaiah 28:16; Zechariah 3:9; 4:7.

The central passage is Matthew 21:42, where our Lord quotes Psalm 118:22 in His parable of the vineyard. It relates to the husbandmen who beat the servants and then killed the heir. Therefore, He said, "The kingdom of God shall be taken from you, and given unto a nation bringing forth the fruits thereof. And whosoever shall fall on this stone shall be broken; but on whomsoever it shall fall, it will grind him to powder."

Later, it is quoted six times in the New Testament, first in relation to the rejection by Israel of their Messiah, and then to the building of the Church, of which Christ is the chief cornerstone, and will be the topstone which will complete the building. Peter tells us that every believer is a living stone in that building (see Acts 4:11; 1 Pet. 2:4-8; Eph. 2:20).

THIS IS THE DAY WHICH THE LORD HATH MADE (V. 24)

The greatest day in Israel's calendar year was the Day of Atonement (Yom Kippur), described in Leviticus 16, and expounded in Hebrews 9. It was the day when sin was confessed and removed by the blood of the sin offering. It typified and pointed forward to another day, when one sacrifice forever was offered on Calvary's cross by God's Lamb, our Lord Jesus Christ. But this also looks ahead to a day in the future when the nation of Israel will look on Him whom they pierced. When they see Him, at His appearing in glory, with the marks of crucifixion upon His Person, for the first time, nationally, they will realize the enormity of their sin and guilt.

They will separate into tribes and families, and as individuals will truly repent. In the language of Isaiah 53, they will then confess their sin. A fountain will be opened for sin and for uncleanness, and a nation will be born in a day (Zech. 12:10-13:1). It will be the final fulfillment of the Day of Atonement.

HOSANNA, BLESSED BE HE THAT COMETH IN THE NAME OF THE LORD (VV. 25-26)

In the early part of Passion Week, when the Lord went up to the Temple as King, the fickle crowd cried: "Hosanna... Blessed is He that cometh in the name of the Lord"; but a few days later, as the shadows began to lengthen and the cross drew near, as He left the doomed city, He cried: "O Jerusalem, Jerusalem, thou that killest the prophets, and stonest them that are sent unto thee, how often would I have gathered thy children together, even as a hen gathereth her chickens under her wings, and ye would not! Behold, your house is left unto you desolate. For I say unto you, ye shall not see Me henceforth, till ye shall say, Blessed is He that cometh in the name of the Lord" (Mt. 23:37-39). Two thousand years have intervened since that day, and Israel as a nation is still in unbelief and blindness of heart. The veil is still on their eyes and minds, but one day it will be lifted when this Scripture is fulfilled.

NATIONAL CONVERSION (V. 27)

"God is the Lord, which hath showed us light." Kay has suggested that the "light" here is the return of the Shekinah glory. But it may have another meaning.

The Apostle Paul, in 1 Timothy 1:15-16, tells us that his conversion on the Damascus road was a pattern *(hupotuposin)* to them which hereafter should believe on Him to life everlasting. What happened to him individually was a delineation of that which would happen to Israel nationally. Again and again he refers to that light, brighter than the sun, which blinded him when he was on his wild career to persecute the saints. He testified to King Agrippa that he was commissioned "to open their eyes, and to turn them from darkness to light, and from the power of Satan unto God, that they may receive forgiveness of sins, and inheritance among them that are sanctified." As in the case of Thomas, who said: "Except I ...see...I will not believe," a sight of the risen Christ, with the nail prints in His hands and feet and the spear wound in His side, turned doubt and unbelief into worshiping faith, when he cried, "My Lord and my God." So it will be with Israel in that day. They shall look on Him whom they pierced, and after repentance and forgiveness, will be restored to relationship with Jehovah.

THE FESTAL SACRIFICE (V. 27)

"Bind the sacrifice with cords, even unto the horns of the altar." The foundation of all these blessings is the atoning work of Christ on the cross. The usual word for "sacrifice" in the Old Testament is *zebach.* But the word used here is *chag.* It is the frequently used word for "feast," the feast of the Passover, Pentecost, and Tabernacles. It has to do with the sacrifices offered at these feasts. In this sense, it occurs 52 times, but only three times is rendered "sacrifice." See Exodus 23:18, the only place where it occurs in the Pentateuch. It means "a festal sacrifice."

If it is true that this was the hymn sung in the upper room at the passover supper and the institution of the Lord's Supper, what solemn light it throws on the thoughts in the mind of our Lord, as He went out to Gethsemane and the cross.

It was the Passover season. Families and bands of pilgrims would be converging on the city, each family with a paschal lamb. Tradition says that the lamb had a garland of flowers around its neck, but when it came to the altar, the garland was taken off and tied to the horns of the altar, when the lamb was sacrificed and death took place.

At that last passover season, we read of our Lord being bound five times: in Gethsemane (Jn. 18:12). Judas was responsible for this, having betrayed the One who had offered him His eternal friendship; by Annas, who sent Him to Caiphas (Jn. 18:24); by the elders and chief priests, and sent to Pilate (Mt. 27:2; Mk. 15:1); by Pilate who "took Jesus, and scourged Him" (Jn. 19:1); and by the nails to the cross.

It is always a bitter moment for a prisoner when the officers of the law bind him. Paul speaks of Onesiphorus as a man who "was not ashamed of my chain." Our Lord felt most acutely the disgrace of prison shackles. When first bound in the garden, He remonstrated: "Are ye come out as against a [petty] thief, with swords and with staves to take Me?"

But it was the cords of love divine which bound the festal sacrifice to the altar. First, love for the will of God. He could say, "Not My will but Thine be done." Secondly, love for the Word of God: "that the Scriptures might be fulfilled." Thirdly, for the joy set before Him, He endured the cross (Heb. 12:1-2). Finally, like the Hebrew servant (Ex. 21), He could say, "I love my Master, I love my wife, I love my children. I will not go out free."

THE FINAL BENEDICTION (VV. 28-29)

"Thou art my God, and I will praise Thee: Thou art my God, I will exalt Thee. O give thanks unto the Lord; for He is good: for His mercy endureth for ever."

Bibliography

Alexander, William. *The Witness of the Psalms to Christ and Christianity.* London: John Murray, 1877.

Bellett, J. G. *Short Meditations on the Psalms.* London: G. Morrish, 1910.

Clarke, Arthur G. *Analytical Studies in the Psalms.* Kilmarnock, Scotland: John Ritchie, 1949.

Gaebelein, Arno C. *The Book of Psalms: A Devotional and Prophetic Commentary.* Neptune, New Jersey: Loizeaux Brothers, 1939, 1965.

Gilford, E. H. *The Authorship of the 110th Psalm.* London: Longmans, Green, 1911.

Grant, F. W. *The Numerical Bible: The Psalms.* Neptune, New Jersey: Loizeaux Brothers, 1897.

Ironside, H. A. *Studies on Book One of the Psalms.* Neptune, New Jersey: Loizeaux Brothers, 1952.

Kay, W. *The Psalms.* Oxford: T. and G. Shrimpton, 1864.

Maclaren, Alexander. *The Book of Psalms.* (3 volumes) London: Hodder and Stoughton, 1891.

Pettingill, William L. *Christ in the Psalms.* Wheaton, Illinois: Van Kampen Press, 1937.

Pridham, Arthur. *Notes and Reflections on the Psalms.* London:

James Nesbit, 1869.

Reich, Max Isaac. *The Messianic Hope of Israel.* Chicago: Moody Press, 1945.

—*Studies in the Psalms of Israel.* Harrisburg, Pennsylvania: Christian Publications, 1967.

Sauer, Erich. *The King of the Earth.* London: Paternoster Press, 1962.

Scroggie, W. Graham. *A Guide to the Psalms.* Grand Rapids, Michigan: Kregel, 1995.

Spurgeon, C. H. *The Treasury of David.* (3 volumes) Peabody, MA: Hendrickson, 1990.

Stott, John R. W. *The Canticles and Selected Psalms.* London: Hodder and Stoughton, 1966.

Appendix 1
A Daily Reading Schedule

A suggested scheme to read through the Psalms in one month.

DAY	FIVE PSALMS TO BE READ EACH DAY				
1	1	31	61	91	121
2	2	32	62	92	122
3	3	33	63	93	123
4	4	34	64	94	124
5	5	35	65	95	125
6	6	36	66	96	126
7	7	37	67	97	127
8	8	38	68	98	128
9	9	39	69	99	129
10	10	40	70	100	130
11	11	41	71	101	131
12	12	42	72	102	132
13	13	43	73	103	133
14	14	44	74	104	134
15	15	45	75	105	135
16	16	46	76	106	136
17	17	47	77	107	137
18	18	48	78	108	138
19	19	49	79	109	139
20	20	50	80	110	140
21	21	51	81	111	141
22	22	52	82	112	142
23	23	53	83	113	143
24	24	54	84	114	144
25	25	55	85	115	145
26	26	56	86	116	146
27	27	57	87	117	147
28	28	58	88	118	148
29	29	59	89	119	149
30	30	60	90	120	150

Psalm 119 could be kept as the reading for Day 31.

Appendix 2
Figures of Speech in the Psalms

The following are only a few of the more common figures of speech among the hundreds in the Psalms.

1. *Allegory:* detailed description of one thing under the image of another. Differs from a metaphor or simile in that these generally have only one point of comparison with the object in question. A good example of allegory is Israel's portrayal as a Vine in Psalm 80:8-16.

2. *Metaphor:* Comparison by representation. The comparison is implied, not expressed, where one thing is spoken for another. See Psalm 84:11, "The Lord God is a sun and shield."

3. *Simile:* Comparison by resemblance. Actually likening one thing with another with the use of "like" or "as." Psalm 1:3-4 states: "He shall be like a tree.... The ungodly...are like the chaff."

4. *Metonomy:* A figure by which one word is put for another because there is some actual relation between them. "Thou shalt eat the labor of thine hands" (the food your hands cultivated).

5. *Synecdoche:* Where the whole is taken for a part or a part is taken for the whole. See Psalm 52:4, "Thou lovest all devouring words, O thou deceitful tongue." Here the tongue stands for the man who uses it in this way.

6. *Hyperbole:* When more is said than is literally meant; exaggeration for effect. "All the night make I my bed to swim," speaking of his great sorrow. (See Ps. 6:6.)

7. *Personification:* A figure by which intelligence is attribut-

ed to inanimate objects or abstract ideas. In Psalm 35:10, synecdoche is used first and then personification: "All my bones shall say, Lord, who is like unto Thee?" The bones are first taken for the whole man and then they begin to speak!

8. *Apostrophe:* Where inanimate objects are addressed. See Psalm 114:5 for an illustration, "What ailed thee, O thou sea, that thou fleddest? thou Jordan, that thou wast driven back?"

9. *Anthropomorphism:* Where human language is used of God to help understand Him better. He is represented as having feet, hands, a face, etc., and is said to laugh, shout, walk, look, etc. These do not make His actions any less real by transferring them into human language.

Appendix 3
Other Groupings of Psalms

Rather than trying to study all 150 psalms in one category, you may like to study them under various groupings. The *Messianic* Psalms, dealt with in this study, are obviously not the only such grouping. For example:

1. The *Penitential* Psalms record sorrow over sin and the subsequent joy of forgiveness, including: Psalms 6, 32, 38, 51, 102, 130, 143. These can be used to manifest the anatomy of a sin—its causes, its warnings, its damage, and steps necessary for restoration.

2. The *Alphabetical* or *Acrostic* Psalms, of which Psalm 119 is the most famous, are an interesting collection: Psalms 9, 10, 25, 34, 37, 111, 112, 119, 145. Of course there are other acrostic sections of Scripture: the Virtuous Woman passage in Proverbs 31, and the five poems of the Lamentations. The acrostic form is not complete in many of these passages (is that poetic licence?). No doubt the form was originally an aid to memorizing, but their careful construction, like counted cross-stitch, can still be admired for their beauty.

3. The *Hallel* (Praise) Psalms, a mini-hymnbook within the Psalms, were used by the Jews on special occasions: Psalms 113-118.

4. The *Historical* Psalms are as follows (taken from their titles): Psalms 3, 7, 18, 30, 34, 51, 52, 54, 56, 57, 59, 60, 63, 142. Many of these form an interesting study when compared with the historical setting in 2 Samuel and elsewhere. One important question: what lessons did the psalmist learn from this trial?

5. The Songs of *Degrees* or *Ascents* (Psalms 120-134) were obviously designed for the people of God to use in connection with their temple worship. For an interesting discussion of the design and purpose of this group, see W. Graham Scroggie's section in his book on the Psalms.

6. The *Imprecatory* Psalms, calling for the invoking of evil upon others, have caused much consternation among the Lord's people since they clearly seem to be contrary to the spirit of grace. They are: Psalms 35, 55, 58, 59, 69, 83, 109, 137, 140. Many suggestions have been made as to explanations; one helpful idea is that the Psalms is the hymnbook of the ages and God has seen to it that every period in history has a selection of psalms to use. This collection is in fact the hymnbook of the Remnant during the Tribulation, the only words fitting that grievous situation. If so, how it should spur us on to evangelize the Jews and to pray for the peace of Jerusalem.

Scripture Index